The Elegant Taste of Thailand
Cha Am Cuisine

Cha-Am is a district town in Phetburi, an old province which has long played a prominent role in Thai history.

Phetburi was a center of civilization at an early date and at one time was the seat of kings. It has its own distinctive art and culture as well as the natural beauty of its hills and sea coasts. It is little wonder, then, that it is famed as a tourist destination. Among the local products are Phetburi rose apples, sugar, and a variety of sweets, among which **mo kaeng,** a type of custard, is perhaps the favorite.

Cha-Am itself is noted as a seaside resort. The reason is the long, clean beaches of fine, white sand and the magnificent expanse of tropical green sea lapping against them. The sunrises there are unforgettable. These attractions make Cha-Am a wonderful place to escape the heat and relax by the sea enjoyed by both Thais themselves and their guests from abroad.

The Elegant Taste of Thailand
Cha Am Cuisine

SLG BOOKS
Berkeley / Hong Kong

First published November 1989 by

SLG BOOKS
P.O. BOX 9465
BERKELEY, CA 94709
Tel: (510) 841-5525
Fax (510) 841-5537

Second Printing: September 1990
Third Printing: July 1991
Fourth Printing: October 1992

Photographs by:
Sangwan Phrathep
Wisit Makham
Chaiyot Uluchada
Roger Williams

Cover: Yuk Wah Lee

Editor: Roger Williams

Typography: Mark Weiman/Regent Press

Color separations and printing by
Snow Lion Graphics
Berkeley/Hong Kong

Library of Congress Cataloging-in-Publication Data

Sisamon Kongpan.
The Elegant Taste of Thailand: Cha Am Cuisine/by Sisamon
Kongpan and Pinyo Srisawat.
   p. cm
Includes index.
ISBN 0-943389-05-4
1. Cookery, Thai.   2. Cookery-Thailand-Cha-am.
I. Pinyo Srisawat, 1956-   II. Title.
TX724.5.T5S57   1989
641.59593 – dc20   89-10050
                                                    CIP

ISBN 0-943389-05-4

CONTENTS

NOTE FROM THE EDITOR
8

INTRODUCTION
9

CURRY PASTES
23

APPETIZERS
29

SOUPS
55

SALADS
68

MAIN DISHES
92

SWEETS & DRINKS
203

INDEX
218

ASIAN MARKETS LISTING
224

A NOTE FROM THE EDITOR

In the process of editing the English text of *THE ELEGANT TASTE OF THAILAND* a few helpful hints for the reader came to mind. I'd like to share these with you.

All transliteration can be somewhat confusing, all the more so if one does not speak the primary language involved. Different people, including professionals, will spell the same foreign word a variety of ways in English. Please don't allow these different renderings into English to annoy or confuse you. After all, an attempt is being made to reproduce words from Thai whose sounds do not exist in the English lanugage. So when next you go to a Thai restaurant and see the word for chicken written as 'gai' and yet in this cook book it is written as 'kai', fear not, for it is the same word. Other examples follow: tod-thot, man-mun, kaeng-gaeng, rat-lad, pha naeng-panang, tom-dom, matsaman-mussaman, thot-tod, pet-ped and so on. I have seen tom yan kun, perhaps Thailand's most well known soup spelled at least a half a dozen similar but different ways.

As authenticity was the major impetus behind the creation of this Thai cook book, we have retained the traditional ingredients as dictated by one of Thailand's foremost exponents in the field of Siamese culinary art. Therefore, if the recipe calls for fresh coriander (cilentro) root, then fresh coriander root it is. We apologize for any temporary inconvenience this may cause our readers, but we feel that the effort is well worth the results.

What makes Thai food unique is the combination and balance of ingredients. If subsitutions must be made, then we request that you be vigilant in making use of our thoroughly annotated and well illustrated introduction. (pp. 9-21).

A good example would be the cucumber. When a particular recipe calls for 10 cucumbers, we mean "cucumber" as defined by *THE ELEGANT TASTE OF THAILAND*, described on page 21 of the introduction, i.e. "short fruits about 8cm (3 ins)long". Obviously we do not mean 10 cucumbers, 8 inches long, 5 inches in circumference, weighing 1/4 lb each. Why do we do this, you ask? We do this because the resultant taste will be more authentically Thai. Needless to say, you can substitute American or English cucumbers, but we ask you to take size and weight into consideration when you must implement substitutions.

The same can be said of celery. Chinese celery is much smaller and has a far stronger taste than our local celery. Therefore, when a recipe calls for "1 celery plant", we mean "celery plant" as described on page 18 and illustrated on page 20. When the recipe for Stuffed Cabbage instructs us to "Immerse the stalks in boiling water until flexable enough to be used for tying the cabbage leaves closed", we mean "celery stalks" as defined by *THE ELEGANT TASTE OF THAILAND*.

At the end of this book you will find a listing of Thai food markets across the United States. Feel free to contact these markets for assistance in obtaining difficult to acquire ingredients. Likewise, feel free to contact us at SLG BOOKS if any problems arise in your pursuit for expertise in the art of Thai cuisine.

Good luck and good eating.

Roger Williams, Editor

INTRODUCTION

Thai cooking is an artform. Before I write about the recipes themselves, we need to generate a sense of it's overall process. Maybe the word "rice" creates a definite image or sensation for you. There are hardly any meals served in Thailand where there is not rice. It is the basis of our diet. If you observe "rice" carefully you will see that it has a certain absorbtive quality. It is also very malleable, and easy to store. It can be dished up quickly; and combined with many dishes, absorbing their flavors. On the dinner table there might be as many as twenty courses of meat, vegetables, fish and fruit dishes, which can be combined in any combination desired with one's rice. In this way, the rice always has the taste of the chosen dish. This is the reason the Thai's never tire of rice. The rice and it's complimentary dish become one-like yang and yin.

You could say that cooking is like a meditation. One needs to be focused in a calm way in order to surmount the barriers for reaching one's goal of a near-perfect meal. We do not need lopsided and oversized vegetables and bulgy-fatty pieces of meat. Another barrier is the desire to use an over-abundance of spices. It comes from a fear that one will not be able to taste the meal and a mistrust of recipes.

Actually there is considerable skill, know-how and even mythology involved in the cooking process. In Thailand we often use a section of the trunk of a tamarind tree as a chopping block. There are many cooks who believe that this will add to the ultimate flavor of the finished product. It is true that one cannot be an expert Thai cook without considerable practice at cutting, as well as focusing on the actual process going on in the cooking utensil. The meat should be sliced into even, small or thin pieces. Vegetables are cut at an angle and in much the same way. It seems that every chef has his or her own idiosyncrasies about cutting, but there are some basics that most of us will agree on. We will all agree that fish, for example, is scored (cut slightly sometimes in patterns) just before steaming. This allows the herbs and spieces which garnish the fish to permeate it's flesh. To empower the fish with your own flair and artistery will be a matter of style and focus.

One of the little secrets of our cooking process is the use of spices. Take a coriander seed, for example, it is a small seed about the size of a beebee, and it seems just as hard. If you put the seeds in a dry frying pan or wok, they will roast and become soft. But, then, if one crushes the seed before roasting, one will immediately smell the delicious aroma. If you cook the seeds in a pan that has a little oil eventually the seed will burst and release the flavor. However, the oil may blacken during the time it takes to burst the seeds. This will give your cooking a burnt taste: this is a no-no. It depends on how you want to release the flavor. The same idea applies to almost any seed, which is one of the reasons the mortar and pestle is so popular. Sometimes you will want to crush the seeds for the purpose of making a paste. The important point for cooking seeds is that the heat, whatever·type, should be low. As they are being cooked the seeds should be constantly turned. If one has a wok, a large metal spatula that is curved to fit the side of the rounded wok will be used.

The wok is the utensil par exellence for the production, control and distribution of heat. For those who have never seen a wok before, I like to describe it as an upside-down iron hat. Imagine the perimeter of the hat expanded twice the size of your head; take it off and place it on a metal ring on the coals or stove. If you want to buy an authentic wok go to a Thai or any oriental grocery. There are different sizes of woks; choose one that fits your cooking needs.

First of all, the wok needs to be cleaned and dried. This is a very important first step because sometimes the manufacturer coats the metal with a protective substance. The rest is simple: rub both the outside and inside with vegetable oil and then place the wok in an oven at about 350 degrees for around two hours. Then, after turning off the oven, let the wok cool down in the oven-the wok has been seasoned, a kind of cooking process in itself. A great reason to have a finely seasoned wok is that you will not have to use as much oil. Season your wok well;, and never use more than two tablespoons of oil, and just use common sense in the amount of food you want to cook at the same time.

Steaming is another form of Thai cooking. Once you have decided that this is a good way to cook, you can invest in a steamer. There are metal and bamboo steamer trays. The bamboo ones will fit inside your wok. Because the water and it's steam will remove the layer of seasoning formed on the surface of the wok, it is a little awkward to always have to re-season the utensil. But, you can also purchase metal trays with a seperate steamer pot. They are very practical.

If your steam trays warp or lose their shape they will not fit on top of each other. This is enough to give up steaming. Store the trays in a spot where the rims will not be damaged. It is very important to put enough water in your wok. If your water boils away, guess what happens to your wok? Steaming is fun. You can reload your trays over and over again; all that is needed is a steady stream of steam and plenty of food. Fill your wok or pot at least three-quarters full of water, and do not remove the lid or the trays until you are almost sure the food is done.

Now that you have an insider's look at the meditative process of Thai cooking you are ready for some images of rice, flour, noodles, sugars and so on. This will help you in purchasing your groceries in Thai and other oriental food stores.

RICE

Rice, khao jao, ข้าวเจ้า, the staple food in the central and southern parts of Thailand, is long-grained, nonglutinous rice. Uncooked grains are translucent; when cooked, the rice is white and fluffy.

Glutinous rice, khao niao, ข้าวเหนียว, also known as sticky rice, is the mainstay of the diet in the northern and northeastern regions of the country and is used in confections in all regions. Uncooked grains are starchy white in color.

Fermented rice, khao mak, ข้าวหมาก, is made by fermenting cooked glutinous rice and is sold as a sweet.

Rice-pot crust, khao tang, ข้าวตัง, is the crust which sometimes forms at the bottom of the pot in which rice is cooked. This is dried in the sun. Dried pot crust is available in the market. It is fried before eating.

FLOUR

Rice flour, paeng khao jao, แป้งข้าวเจ้า, is made from nonglutinous rice.

Glutinous rice flour, paeng khao niao, แป้งข้าวเหนียว, is made from glutinous rice.

Corn flour, paeng khao phot, แป้งข้าวโพด, is a fine white flour made from corn.

Tapioca pellets ,sa-khu met lek, สาคูเม็ดเล็ก, are the tiny balls (about 2 mm in diameter) made from tapioca, some used in sweets. They should be mixed with hot, but not scalding, water and kneaded, and then allowed to stand for a time covered with a damp cloth to permit the water to penetrate to the core.

Wheat flour, paeng sa-li, แป้งสาลี, may be general purpose flour unless cake flour is specified.

Tapioca flour, paeng man sampalang, แป้งมันสำปะหลัง, is made from tapioca, or cassava, tubers. When this or any of the other flour is used to thicken a sauce, it is first mixed well with a little water so that it will not lump in the sauce.

NOODLES

Rice noodles, kuai-tiao, เส้นก๋วยเตี๋ยว, are flat white noodles made from rice flour and are cut into strips of three widths: **wide** (2-3 cm), sen yai, เส้นใหญ่, **narrow** (about 5 mm), sen lek, เส้นเล็ก, and **thin** (1-2 mm), sen mi, เส้นหมี่, uncut fresh noodles sheets are sold in the market, as are fresh wide and narrow rice noodles. Thin noodles are available dried, and wide and narrow noodles may also be bought in this form. Dried noodles are soaked in water before use to soften them.

Vermicelli, khanom jin, ขนมจีน are thin, round noodles, also made from rice flour, and sold fresh in the form of wads that look like birds' nests. They should be eaten within a few days of being made, and it is a good practice to steam them after bringing them home from the market.

Egg noodles, ba mi, บะหมี่, are yellow noodles made from wheat flour. Small balls of this kind of noodles are available in the market.

Mungbean noodles, wun sen, วุ้นเส้น, are thread-like noodles made from mung bean flour. They are sold dried and are soaked in water before use. When cooked, they become transparent. High quality noodles maintain their integrity in soup better than do cheap ones.

SUGARS

Sugar, nam tan sai, น้ำตาลทราย, is granulated cane sugar. Colors range from white to reddish and textures from fine to coarse. Some people find the reddish sugar tastier than the more highly refined white. The cleanliness of sugars in the market varies so it is wise to inspect carefully for foreign matter before purchase. Even so, some debris, such as tiny threads of cane, may remain and thus the recipes call for the straining of sugar solutions when clarity is desired.

Palm sugar, nam tan pip, น้ำตาลปีบ, was originally made from the sap of the sugar, or palmyra, palm, *Borassus flabellifera*, called tan in Thai, which has a very rough trunk and large, fan-shapped leaves. Now it is generally made from the sap of coconut palms, and may be sold as coconut sugar. The sugar is a light goldenbrown paste with a distinctive flavor and fragrance. It is put up in five-gallon kerosene cans, called pip in Thai.

ANIMAL PRODUCTS

Fish sauce, nam pla, น้ำปลา, is a clear, brown liquid derived from a brew of fish or shrimp mixed with salt. It is sold in bottles and plastic jugs as well as in earthenware jars. High quality fish sauce has a fine aroma and taste. Fish sauce is placed on the table as a condiment at nearly every meal, either as is or mixed with sliced chillies and perhaps lime juice.

Salted fish, pla khem, ปลาเค็ม, is dried, salted sea fish, such as pla insee, ปลาอินทรี. In the market, the seller will cut you a steak of the required thickness. This is slowly roasted for a time to bring out the aroma.

Dried fish, pla haeng, ปลาแห้ง, is a freshwater fish, such as serpent head, which is slit open, gutted, and spread to dry in the sun.

Shrimp paste, ka-pi, กะปิ, is shrimp which are salted, perhaps brewed for a time, allowed to dry in the sun, then ground and worked with the addition of moisture into a fine-textured puce paste, which is fragrant and slightly salty.

Dried shrimp, kung haeng, กุ้งแห้ง, are small shrimp which have been dried in the sun. The quality product is plump orange and whitish shrimp with a minimum of debris.

Mackerel, pla thu, ปลาทู, is a small saltwater fish, *Rastrelliger chrysozonus* (Scombridae). Steamed mackerel in small woven trays are sold in food shops nearly everywhere in the country; **fresh mackerel,** pla thu sot, ปลาทูสด, are available at the fishmonger's in the market.

Sea perch, pla kaphong, ปลากะพง, is a general name for fish of the sea bass and sea perch families.

Rock cod, pla kao, ปลาเก๋า, is also known as grouper, reef cod, and sea bass.

Serpent head, pla chon, ปลาช่อน, is the freshwater fish *Ophiocephalus striatus.*

Featherback, pla krai, ปลากราย, is the freshwater fish *Notopterus chitala.*

Pork belly, mu sam chan, หมูสามชั้น, is bacon-cut pork, with layers of red meat, fat and skin.

Chicken stock, nam sup, น้ำซุป, made from chicken is preferred in Thai cooking. While plain water can substitute, and while the instant chicken broth cubes and pastes marketed by various food manufacturers are certainly fast and convenient. It might be interesting to make up this stock: Chop 3.5 lbs. chicken bones and scrap into 3-4 inch long pieces, place in a pot with 10 cups water and allow to stand 30 minutes. Peel 1 Chinese radishes, cut in half lengthwise and add to pot. Wash 3 celery plants and 3 garlic plants, remove the roots, coil the plants together, tie into a bundle, and add to pot, together with 5 bay leaves and 1 tbsp. salt. Heat to boiling, simmer over low heat for 1-1 ½ hours, and then strain through cheesecloth.

BEANS AND BEAN PRODUCTS

Beancurd, tao hu, เต้าหู้, is made up salted and unsalted in solid and soft forms. The solid curd has a cheesy consistency and is sold in blocks about four inches square. The blocks of the unsalted curd are white while those of the salted, **yellow beancurd,** tao hu leuang, เต้าหู้เหลือง, are yellow on the outside and off-white inside. The solid curd is used in fried dishes. The **soft white beancurd,** tao hu khao chanit on, เต้าหู้ขาวชนิดอ่อน, is cut into bricks for sale and is used in soups.

Fermented soybeans, tao jiao, เต้าเจี้ยว, is a brew of soybeans and salt.

Soybean paste, tao jiao nam, เต้าเจี้ยวน้ำ, is a preparation made with fermented soybeans and flour.

Soy sauces, si-iu, ซีอิ๊ว, used in these

recipes are of the Chinese, rather than the Japanese, type.

Light soy sauce, si-iu khao, ซีอิ๊วขาว, is a clear brown liquid used in much the same way that fish sauce is.

Dark soy sauce, si-iu dam, ซีอิ๊วดำ, is opaque, black, viscous, and sweet. It is mixture of soy sauce and molasses.

Oyster sauce, nam man hoi, น้ำมันหอย, is a sweetened soy sauce to which oyster extract is added.

Black beans, thua dam, ถั่วดำ, are a small dark bean sold dry and used in sweets.

Mungbeans, thua khiao, ถั่วเขียว, are yellow beans with green shells. The shelled bean is used in sweets and the whole bean is sprouted, giving, **bean sprouts,** thua ngok, ถั่วงอก.

Yard-long beans, thua fak yao, ถั่วฝักยาว, have pods up to 60 cm long. These are eaten both fresh and cooked and are at their best when young and slender.

Winged bean, thua phu, ถั่วพู, bears a pod which in cross section looks like a rectangle that has a fringe-like extension at each corner, the ''wings'' of the bean.

HERBS AND SPICES

Ginger, khing, ขิง, *Zingiber officinale,* grows from an underground stem, or rhisome. Mature ginger stems are buff colored; **young or fresh ginger,** khing on, ขิงอ่อน, is white and is eaten fresh and pickled as well as cooked.

Galangal, kha, ข่า, *Alpinia galangal,* is a larger and lighter-colored relative of ginger and has its own distinctive taste.

Krachai, กระชาย, *Kaempferia panduratum,* grows bunches of slender and short yellow-brown tuberous roots and is used in fish dishes.

Turmeric, kha-min, ขมิ้น, *Curcuma longa,* is a small ginger with brown rhisomes. Inside, the flesh is a bright carrot orange. An important use is as a coloring agent.

Lemon grass, ta-khrai, ตะไคร้, *Cymbopgon citratus,* is an aromatic grey-green grass. The bases of the stems are used in cookery.

Garlic, kra-thiam, กระเทียม, *Allium sativum,* is used both by the clove and by the entire bulb. The dry papery skin and the central core should be removed from bulbs. Cloves are often crushed by hitting with a spatula or the side of a knife blade and then the skins are picked out. **Pickled garlic,** kra-thiam dong, กระเทียมดอง, are wonderfully flavorful and can be bought by the bulb or by the jar in the market.

Shallot, hom lek, หอมเล็ก, or hom daeng, หอมแดง, *Allium ascalonicum,* is the zesty small red onion favored in Thai cooking.

Onion, hom hua yai, หอมหัวใหญ่, *Allium cepa,* has light colored bulbs that are larger and milder that those of the shallot.

Cinnamon, op-choey, อบเชย, *Cinnamomum spp.,* is the bark of a number of species of trees in this genus, classified in the laurel family. The types that grow in Southeast Asia are known in commerce as cassias. The barks, which are generally reddish-brown, after being peeled off from around the branch, tend to roll themselves back up, and so have a scroll-like appearance. For retail sale in Thai markets, the bark is cut into stirps about 1 cm across

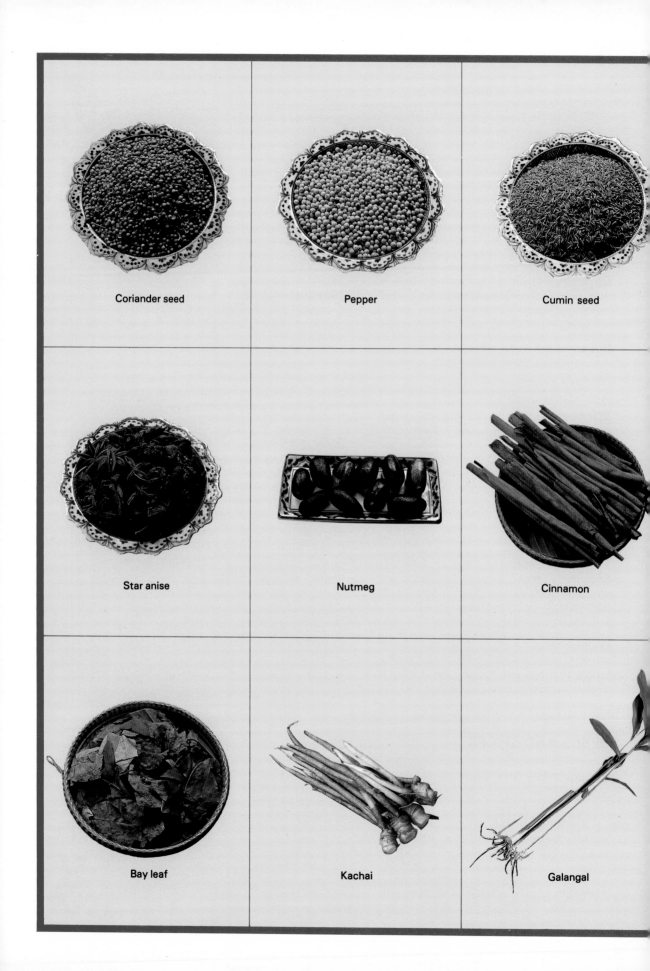

Coriander seed

Pepper

Cumin seed

Star anise

Nutmeg

Cinnamon

Bay leaf

Kachai

Galangal

Chillies

Hot chillies

Dried chillies

Lime

Ginger

Shiitake mushroom

Cherry tomato

Lemon grass

Rice-straw mushroom

and 8-10 cm long, and such strips are the basis for the measurements given in the recipes. Before use, the bark should be roasted to bring out its aroma.

Cloves, kan phlu, กานพลู, are the very fragrant tack-like flower buds of the tree *Caryophyllus aromaticus,* thought to be native to insular Southeast Asia.

Cumin, yi-ra, ยี่หร่า, *Cuminium cyminum,* has elongated yellow-brown seeds about 5 mm in length, which are ridged longitudinally and often have a seed stalk attached. They are roasted before use to heighten their fragrance.

Sesame, nga, งา, *Sesamum indium,* has small oval seeds which are white and have dark hulls. They are usually sold hulled.

Cardamoms, luk kra-wan, ลูกกระวาน, *Amomum krevanh,* appear like miniature unhusked coconuts. The off-white, bulb-shaped capsules reach about 1 cm in length and slightly more than this in diameter. Inside is a densely-packed cluster of angular, dark brown seeds, which are aromatic and have a slightly hot taste.

Bay leaf, bai kra-wan, ใบกระวาน, is an elliptical leaf about 7 cm long, greygreen on the bottom, having a brownish cast on the top, which is sold dried in the market.

Coriander, phak chi, ผักชี, *Coriandrum sativum,* is of the parsley family. The leaves and stems are eaten fresh and used frequently as a garnish. The root and the seeds are ingredients in many dishes. The root is taken from the fresh plant. The seeds which are roughly spherical, 2-4 cm in diameter, and range in color from off-white to brown, have a pleasant taste and fragrance. They can be bought in the market. It is better to roast and grind seeds immediately before use than

to buy ground coriander seed.

Sweet basil ,maenglak, แมงลัก, is a bright light green plant with a tangy taste.

Sweet basil ,horapha, โหระพา, is an attractive plant with deep green leaves and often reddish stems. It has a taste reminiscent of anise.

Pepper, phrik thai, พริกไทย, *Piper nigrum;* produces berries, which, when ripe, are dried and ground with the skins on to give black pepper, or with the skins off to give white pepper. The most widely available form in Thailand is white pepper.

Chillies, phrik, พริก, *Capsicum annuum,* of several varieties are available in Thailand. As they ripen, they change color from green to red and become hotter. Fully ripe fruits are dried in the sun to give **dried chillies,** phrik haeng, พริกแห้ง, and these are pounded for **ground dried chilli,** phrik pon, พริกป่น.

Hot chillies, phrik khi nu, พริกขี้หนู, are the hottest type and also the smallest, being only about a centimeter long.

Pandanus leaf, bai toey, ใบเตย, *Pandanus odorus,* the long, bright green leaf of a small palm and is used in making sweets.

FRUITS AND VEGETABLES

Eggplant, ma-kheua, มะเขือ, *Solanum spp,* are eaten with nam phrik. There are a number of types, ranging in size from that of a ping-pong ball down to that of a marble, in shape from that of an egg to that of a flattened sphere, and in color from green and white to yellow. One small type is called **ma-kheua pro,** มะเขือเปราะ.

Ma-kheua phuang, มะเขือพวง, *Solanum torvum,* grow in clusters and, when yet unripe, look like large peas.

Long eggplant, ma-kheua yao, มะเขือยาว, has a long green fruit.

Banana, Nam Wa variety, kluai nam wa, กล้วยน้ำว้า, *Musa sapientum,* probably the most popular eating banana among the nearly thirty varieties found in Thailand, has short oblong fruits that become a pale yellow as they ripen. The leaf, bai tong, ใบตอง, of this variety is used in Glutinous Rice Wrapped in Banana Leaf. Wrapping goes more easily if the sections are torn and allowed to stand overnight before wrapping.

Coconut, ma-phrao, มะพร้าว, *Cocos nucifera,* is found nearly everywhere people have settled in all parts of the country and its production is important to the economy. The use to coconut milk in curries is a hallmark of Thai cooking. The meat of ripe nuts is scraped either by hand or by machine. The grated coconut is placed in a basin and mixed with a certain amount of warm water. The coconut is then picked up in the hand, held over a second container, and squeezed to press out the **coconut milk,** ka-thi, กะทิ. A fine-meshed strainer should be positioned below the hand during squeezing to catch any meat that falls. Many cooks add a little salt to the water or the milk.

Coconut cream, hua ka-thi, หัวกะทิ, can be obtained by mixing a little warm water with the grated coconut and collecting the required amount of cream on the first squeezing. Following this, water can be added again and the grated coconut can be squeezed a second and a third time to obtain a less rich milk, which is kept separate from the cream. Alternatively, the full amount of warm water may be

mixed with the grated coconut. After squeezing, the liquid is allowed to stand for a time, and then the cream is skimmed from top with a spoon.

Fastidious cooks scrape mature brown coconuts themselves by hand and coconut thus grated is usually pure white. In the market, however, the work is done with a machine that accepts chunks of coconut cut from the shell and usually a thin layer of shell still adheres to the meat. As a result, the grated coconut sold in the market is flecked with tiny brown particles of shell. This is useable for making coconut milk but is unacceptable when the grated coconut itself is to be used, for example, as a topping for a sweet. For such purposes, the recipes specify **white grated coconut,** ma-phrao khao, มะพร้าวขาว, which is also available in the market.

For the sake of efficiency in extracting coconut milk, grated coconut is quite fine, but in making sweets, a coarser cut is sometimes desired. This **shredded coconut,** ma-phrao theun theuk khut kratai jin, มะพร้าวทึนทึกขูดกระต่ายจีน, is sold in the market and is obtained by using a special scraper. This lacking, the top of a soft drink bottle might be used to scrape threads of coconut meat.

For those who wish to avoid the bother of scraping and squeezing, ready-made coconut milk is offered by food processors. This can be used in the recipes simply by measuring out the amount specified. In recipes which distinguish coconut cream from coconut milk, coconut cream is approximated by the ready-made coconut milk used full strength right from the container, while coconut milk may be approximated by mixing one part of the ready-made product with one part water.

Lime, ma-nao, มะนาว, *Citrus acida,* has small spherical fruits which are green or yellow. Lemon may be used.

Kaffir lime, ma-krut, มะกรูด, *Citrus hy-*

Baby corn

Sponge gourd

Wax gourd

Chinese cabbage

Yard-long bean

Long eggplant

Celery

Swamp cabbage

Sweet basil *(maeng lak)*

Spring onion

Chinese chive

Coconut

Garlic plant

Mint

Ma-kheua phuang

Ma-kheua pro

Sweet basil *(horapha)*

Coriander

strix, has green fruits with wrinkled skin. The rind and the leaves are used in cookery.

Tamarind, ma-kham, มะขาม, *Tamarindus indica,* is a tree which bears tan pods inside of which are bean-like hard brown seeds surrounded by sticky flesh. The tan pod shell can be removed easily. **Ripe tamarind,** ma-kham piak, มะขามเปียก, is the flesh, seeds, and veins, of several fruit pressed together in the hand to form a wad.

Tamarind juice, nam som ma-kham, น้ำส้มมะขาม, is obtained by mixing some of the ripe fruit with water and squeezing out the juice. The immature fruit and the young leaves and flowers are also used, all to give a sour taste. There are also sweet tamarinds which are a delight to eat and command a high price.

Mushrooms, het, เห็ด, of many types are available fresh. The most common is the **rice straw mushroom,** het fang, เห็ดฟาง.

Ear mushroom, het hu nu, เห็ดหูหนู, is a dark greyish brown fungus that has a delightful crunchy texture.

Shiitake mushroom, het hom, เห็ดหอม, is available dried in the market.

Spring onion, ton hom, ต้นหอม, *Allium fistulosum,* also called green onion or scallion, has leaves that are circular in cross section. These are much used as a garnish. The bases of the plant are frequently served on the side of one-dish meals, such as fried rice, or placed on the salad plate.

Garlic plant, ton kra-thiam, ต้นกระเทียม, *Allium sativum,* is the young plant picked before the bulb has formed. The leaves are flat and folded length-wise.

Chinese chives, ton kui chai, ต้นกุยช่าย, *Allium tuberosum,* has fairly thick, narrow, flat leaves which are eaten with fried noodle dishes such as Phat Thai.

Celery, kheun chai, ขึ้นฉ่าย, *Apium graveolens,* also called celeriac, turniprooted celery, or Chinese soup celery, has very small stalks (only a few millimeters across) and a very strong flavor.

Chinese radish, hua phak kat, หัวผักกาด, or hua chai thao, หัวไชเท้า, *Raphanus sativus* (longpinnatus variety), has a long, cylindrical root that looks like a hefty white carrot.

Chinese cabbage, phak kat khao, ผักกาดขาว, *Brassica campestris* (pekinensis variety), has thin, light green leaves and broad, flat, and thin leaf ribs which form an elongated, rather than a spherical, head.

Kale, phak kha-na, ผักคะน้า, *Brassica oleracea* (acephala variety), has leathery grey-green leaves on thick stalks. Stalk lovers buy the large variety, while those partial to the leaves get the dwarf variety.

Chinese mustard green, phak kwang tung, ผักกวางตุ้ง, *Brassica campestris* (chinensis variety), has dark green oval leaves on thick fleshy stalks.

Swamp cabbage, phak bung, ผักบุ้ง, *Ipomoea aquatica,* also called water convolvulus, water spinach, or aquatic morning glory, has hollow stems and roughly triangular leaves. The Thai variety has delicate dark green leaves and deep red stalks while the Chinese is thicker, larger, and lighter green. The tender tips of the stems are eaten fresh or cooked.

Sponge gourd, buap liam, บวบเหลี่ยม,

Luffa acutangula, also called vegetable gourd or Chinese okra, is oblong, pointed, and dark green and has sharp longitudinal ridges.

Wax gourd, fak khiao, ฟักเขียว, *Benincasa hispida,* also called white gourd or Chinese preserving melon, is oblong and light green to white. The ends are rounded and the flesh is solid and white.

Cucumber, taeng kwa, แตงกวา, *Cucumis sativus,* has short fruits about 8 cm long which are crispiest while still green and white, before yellowing. A larger type, taeng ran, แตงร้าน, are also eaten.

Water chestnut, haeo, แห้ว, is the tuber of certain kinds of sedges. The skin is dark and the crunchy meat inside is off-white.

Cha-phlu, ชะพลู, *Piper sarmentosum,* is a creeper with aromatic glossy dark green leaves which resemble those of the betel vine.

Pickled plum, buai dong, บ๊วยดอง, is the preserved fruit of an oriental plum which is sometimes labeled Japanese apricot.

PREPARED SPICE MIXTURES

Five spice powder, phong pha-loh, ผง-พะโล้, is a prepared mixture of spices, among which is star anise, poi-kak, โป๊ย-กั๊ก, *Ilicium verum.*

Curry Powder, phong ka-ri, ผงกะหรี่, is a prepared mixture of spices such as turmeric, coriander seed, ginger, cloves, cinnamon, mustard, cardamom, cumin, chilli, and salt. Each brand has its own character depending on the ingredients used.

DEBONING POULTRY

Bones can be removed from chicken wings by separating the flesh from the bone with a sharp knife and peeling the flesh and skin back. Care should be taken so as not to puncture or tear the flesh.

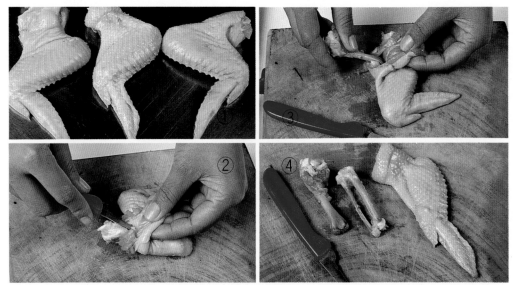

In deboning a duck, a sharp knife with a small, pointed blade is useful. After the duck has been plucked, cleaned, and washed, open the body up from vent to neck and cut and pull the flesh from the bones, trying to leave as little meat as possible on the bones. Remove the neck and work the hands around the ribs and backbone until the skeleton can be lifted free of the flesh. Then, remove the bones from the legs of the duck. Do not puncture or tear the body wall.

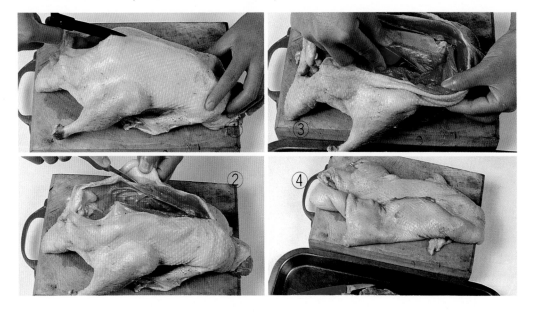

NAM PHRIK PHAO
(Roasted Chili Sauce)

INGREDIENTS :

1/2	cup small dried chillies	8	shallots, sliced
3	tbsp. fish sauce	6	garlic cloves, sliced
2	cups vegetable oil	1	cup dried shrimp
1/3	tsp. salt	1	tbsp. palm sugar
		1 1/2	tbsp. tamarind juce

PREPARATION:

- Heat the oil in a wok and fry the shallots and garlic until golden brown; remove from oil and drain. Add the dried shrimp and dried chillies; fry until golden brown; remove from oil and drain.

- In a mortar or blender, grind the shrimp, garlic, chillies, shallots and sugar until the mixture is blended well. Add the fish sauce, tamarind juice, salt and cooled oil from the wok into the blender; blend until you have a finely textured sauce.

- This can be stored in a glass jar in the refrigerator for about 3-4 months.

Nam Phrik Kaeng Matsaman
(Massaman Curry Paste)

INGREDIENTS :

3	dried chillies, soaked in hot water for 15 minutes and deseeded
3	tbsp. chopped shallots
2	tbsp. chopped garlic
1	tsp. chopped galangal
1 1/4	tbsp. chopped lemon grass
2	cloves
1	tbsp. coriander seeds
1	tsp. cumin seeds
5	pepper corns
1	tsp. shrimp paste
1	tsp. salt

PREPARATION:

- In a wok over low heat put the shallots, garlic, galangal, lemon grass, cloves, coriander seeds, cumin seeds and dry fry for about 5 minutes, then grind into a powder.

- Into a blender, put the rest of the ingredients except the shrimp paste and blend to mix well. Add the shallot-garlic-galangal-lemon grass-clove-coriander seed-cumin seed mixture and the shrimp paste and blend again to obtain 1/2 cup of a fine-textured paste.

- This can be stored in a glass jar in the refrigerator for about 3-4 months.

Nam Phrik Kaeng Ka-ri
(Yellow Curry Paste)

INGREDIENTS :

3	dried chillies, soaked in hot water for 15 minutes and deseeded
3	tbsp. chopped shallots
1	tbsp. chopped garlic
1	tsp. chopped ginger
1	tbsp. coriander seeds
1	tsp. cumin seeds
1	tbsp. chopped lemon grass
1	tsp. shrimp paste
1	tsp. salt
2	tsp. curry powder

PREPARATION:

■ In a wok over low heat, put the shallots, garlic, ginger, coriander seeds and cumin seeds and dry fry for about 5 minutes, then grind into a powder.

■ Into a blender, put the rest of the ingredients and blend to mix well. Add the shallot-garlic-ginger-coriander seed-cumin seed mixture and blend again to obtain about 1/2 cup of a fine-textured paste.

■ This can be stored in a glass jar in the refrigerator for about 3-4 months.

Nam Phrik Kaeng Khua
(Kaeng Khua Curry Paste)

INGREDIENTS :

5	dried chillies, soaked in hot water for 15 minutes and deseeded
3	tbsp. chopped shallots
2	tbsp. chopped garlic
1	tsp. chopped galangal
1	tbsp. chopped lemon grass
1	tsp. chopped kaffir lime rind
1	tsp. chopped coriander root
2	tsp. salt
1	tsp. shrimp paste

PREPARATION:

■ Into a blender, put all ingredients except the shrimp paste and blend until well mixed. Then, add the shrimp paste and blend once more to obtain about 3/4 cup of a fine-textured paste.

■ This can be stored in a glass jar in the refrigerator for about 3-4 months.

Nam Phrik Kaeng Khiao Wan
(Green Curry Paste)

INGREDIENTS :

15	green hot chillies
3	tbsp. chopped shallots
1	tbsp. chopped garlic
1	tsp. chopped galangal
1	tbsp. chopped lemon grass
1/2	tsp. chopped kaffir lime rind
1	tsp. chopped coriander root
5	pepper corns
1	tbsp. coriander seeds
1	tsp. cumin seeds
1	tsp. salt
1	tsp. shrimp paste

PREPARATION:

■ In a wok over low heat, put the coriander seeds, and cumin seeds and dry fry for about 5 minutes, then grind into a powder.

■ Into a blender, put the rest of the ingredients except the shrimp paste and blend to mix well. Add the coriander-cumin seed mixture and the shrimp paste and blend to obtain 1/2 cup of a fine-textured paste.

■ This can be stored in a glass jar in the refrigerator for about 3-4 months.

Nam Phrik Kaeng Som
(Sour Soup Curry Paste)

INGREDIENTS :

7	dried chillies, soaked in hot water for 15 minutes and deseeded
3	tbsp. chopped shallots
1	tbsp. chopped garlic
2	tbsp. chopped krachai
1	tbsp. shrimp paste
1	tsp. salt

PREPARATION:

■ Into a blender, put all ingredients except the shrimp paste and blend until mixed well. Then, add the shrimp paste and blend once more to obtain about 1/2 cup of a fine-textured paste.

■ This can be stored in a glass jar in the refrigerator for about 3-4 months.

Nam Phrik Kaeng Daeng
(Red Curry Paste)

INGREDIENTS :

13	small dried chillies, soaked in hot water for 15 minutes and deseeded
3	tbsp. chopped shallot
4	tbsp. chopped garlic
1	tbsp. chopped galangal
2	tbsp. chopped lemon grass
2	tsp. chopped kaffir lime rind
1	tbsp. chopped coriander root
20	pepper corns
1	tsp. shrimp paste
1	tbsp. coriander seed
1	tsp. cumin seed

PREPARATION:

■ In a wok over low heat, put the coriander seeds and cumin seeds and dry fry for about 5 minutes, then grind into a powder.

■ Into a blender, put the rest of the ingredients except the shrimp paste and blend to mix well. Then add the coriander seed-cumin seed mixture and the shrimp paste and blend again to obtain about 3/4 cup of a fine-textured paste.

■ This can be stored in a glass jar in the refrigerator for about 3-4 months.

Po-Pia Thot
(Egg Rolls)

INGREDIENTS :

1	pack egg-roll sheets
1/2	lb. ground pork
3	oz. crab meat
1	egg
1	3-oz. pack mungbean noodles
1/2	cup shredded carrot
1/2	cup shredded cabbage
1/3	cup (5-6) dried ear mushrooms, chopped (soaked in hot water)
1/2	tbsp. black pepper
1	tbsp. chopped garlic
1/2	tsp. salt
1	tbsp. light soy sauce
3	cups cooking oil

Paste made by mixing 2 tbsp. wheat flour in 1/4 cup water and stirring over low heat.

PREPARATION:

■ Soak the noodles until soft, then cut into short lengths.

■ Mix pork, egg, cabbage, carrots, mushrooms, pepper and light soy sauce together then add the noodles and mix well.

■ Fry the garlic in 3 tbsp. oil and then add the pork and noodle mixture. Fry until fairly dry, then set aside to cool.

■ Place a teaspoonful of the filling on an egg roll sheet, fold the sheet over the filling, fold about half a turn, fold in the ends to close them; then, roll up tightly, sealing the sheet closed with the paste.

■ Deep fry in plenty of oil over low heat until crisp and golden brown.

■ Serve with sauce, sliced cucumber, and sweet basil leaves.

INGREDIENTS FOR EGG ROLL SAUCE :

1/4	cup vinegar
1/4	cup water
1/2	cup sugar
1/2	tsp. salt
1/2	tbsp. chilli, well pounded
2	tsp. tapioca flour mixed in 2 tbsp. water

PREPARATION:

■ Mix the vinegar, water, sugar, salt and chilli; heat to boiling, add a little of the flour water, boil a short time, then remove from heat.

■ Serves six to eight.

Thot Man
(Fish Cakes)

INGREDIENTS :

1 1/2	lb. white fish meat (e.g. ladyfinger), minced or chopped
1	tbsp. red curry paste (see page 26)
1	egg
1/2	cup yard-long beans, minced or chopped
1/3	cup kaffir lime leaves, minced or chopped
1/2	tsp. salt
2	tsp. sugar
3	cups vegetable oil

PREPARATION:

■ Put all the ingredients into a large bowl and mix well with the hand.
■ Shape into small patties about 3" in diameter and deep fry in vegetable oil until golden brown.
■ Serve with peanut sweet chilli sauce.

Peanut Sweet Chilli Sauce

■ Use cucumber relish (see p. 37) and add 1/4 cup sliced shallots and 1/2 cup freshly ground peanuts.
■ Serves four.

Pik Kai Thot
(Fried Stuffed Chicken Wings)

INGREDIENTS :

1	cup breadcrumbs
6	chicken wings, deboned
1	cup mungbean noodles, soaked in warm water for 15 minutes and then cut into 1/2" pieces
1	tbsp. chopped coriander greens
1/2	cup sliced water chestnuts
2	eggs
1	tbsp. chopped garlic
1/3	cup wheat flour
1/2	lb. ground pork

PREPARATION:

■ Mix together the noodles, coriander, chestnuts, one egg, garlic, flour and ground pork and stuff this mixture into the deboned chicken wings (see p. 22) (not too full).

■ Steam the chicken wings for 15 minutes; then, drain and cool. Mix one egg with the breadcrumbs and dip the chicken wings into this mixture and deep fry them until golden brown.

■ Slice and serve with sweet chilli sauce. (See p. 179)

■ Serves four to six.

Mu reu Neua Sa-te
(Pork or Beef Sateh)

INGREDIENTS :

1	lb. pork (or beef)
2	tsp. ground roasted coriander seeds
1/2	tsp. ground roasted cumin seeds
1	tsp. finely chopped galangal
1	heaping tbsp. finely chopped lemon grass
1	tsp. finely chopped turmeric
1/4	tsp. ground pepper
1	tsp. salt
2	tsp. sugar
1/2	cup coconut milk
	bamboo skewers

PREPARATION:

■ Cut the meat into thin slices about 1 inch wide and 2 inches long.

■ Pound the coriander seeds, cumin, galangal, lemon grass, tumeric, salt, and pepper in a mortar until finely ground. Pour over the meat along with the sugar and the coconut milk, mix thoroughly, and set aside to marinate for 30 minutes.

■ Skewer the meat strips lengthwise and broil over a medium charcoal fire, brushing occasionally with the remaining marinade. Serve with sauce and relish.

■ Serves four.

Sateh Sauce

INGREDIENTS :

1/4	cup red curry paste (see page 26)
2	cups coconut milk
1/2	cup creamy peanut butter
1/4	cup sugar
1/4	cup tamarind juice
salt	

Sateh Sauce
(Continued)

PREPARATION:

- Mix the peanut butter and the red curry paste together well.
- Skim one cup of coconut cream from the coconut milk. Heat the coconut cream in a wok until the oil surfaces; then, add the peanut butter-curry paste mixture and stir to mix well. Add the remaining coconut milk and reduce the heat. Continue to stir regularly.
- Season to taste with sugar and tamarind juice, and if you like, with salt. When the sauce has thickened, pour into a serving bowl.

Cucumber Relish

INGREDIENTS :

4	cucumbers (see page 21)
2	shallots
1	chilli
1/3	cup vinegar
2	tsp. sugar
1	tsp. salt

PREPARATION:

- Wash and peel the cucumbers, cut in half lengthwise, and then cut across into thin slices. Cut the shallots and chillies into thin slices. Place the cucumber, shallot, and chilli slices in a bowl.
- Heat the vinegar, sugar, and salt, stirring constantly until sugar has dissolved. When the mixture comes to a boil, remove from the heat. After the mixture has cooled, add it to the bowl and garnish with chopped coriander greens.
- Serves four.

Mu Pan Kon Thot
(Fried Pork Meatballs)

INGREDIENTS :

2	cups ground pork
1	tbsp. well pounded garlic
1	tsp. salt
1	tbsp. fish sauce
2	tbsp. water
1/2	tsp. pepper
2	tsp. well pounded coriander root
1	cup cooking oil

PREPARATION:

■ Mix the pork, salt, fish sauce, pepper, garlic, and coriander root together.

■ Take portions of the mixture of about one tablespoon and form into meatballs.

■ Place the oil in a wok on medium heat. When the oil is hot, fry the meatballs until golden brown; remove and drain.

■ Serve with pineapple, tomato, and spring onions.

■ Serves four.

Thot Man Khao Phot
(Fried Sweet Corn Patties)

INGREDIENTS :

2	cups sweet corn kernels
1/4	tsp. pepper
1	tsp. salt
2	tsp. well-pounded garlic
2	tsp. wheat flour
1	egg
2	cups cooking oil

PREPARATION:

■ Knead together well the corn, pepper, salt, garlic, egg, and flour to obtain a stiff dough.

■ Place the oil in a deep wok over medium heat. When the oil is hot, pick up about 1 tbsp. of the dough, shape into a patty with the fingers, and place the patty in the oil. Continue making patties and putting them in but do not crowd the wok. Turn as needed so the patties brown on both side; then, remove from the oil and drain on absorbent paper.

■ Serve with chilli sauce.

■ Serves four.

Khanom Pang Na Kung Roi Nga

(Fried Canapés with Prawn Spread)

INGREDIENTS :

8	slices bread
1	oz. prawns
4	oz. lean pork
1	egg
1	tsp. thinly sliced coriander root
5	cloves garlic
1/8	tsp. pepper
2	tsp. light soy sauce
1/4	tsp. salt
2	tbsp. white sesame seeds
3	cups cooking oil

PREPARATION:

- Dry the bread in a low temperature oven. Alternatively, use bread which has dried out, for this will absorb less oil and give you very crisp canapés.
- Shell and clean the prawns, add the pork, and mince.
- Remove the skins of the garlic cloves, place in a mortar with the coriander root and pepper, and pound to a fine paste.
- Knead the pounded garlic mixture together with the minced pork and prawn; then, add the egg and knead once again until uniform in consistency.
- Divide the mixture into eight portions and spread one portion on each slice of bread. Smooth the surface of the spread and sprinkle with about 1/2 tsp. seasame seeds.
- Heat the oil in a deep wok. When it is hot, fry each slice of bread spread-side down · When the spread has become golden brown, remove the bread from the oil and drain on absorbent paper.
- Cut each slice of bread into quarters, arrange on a serving platter, and seve with marmalade sauce or maggi sauce and fresh vegetables, such as chilled cucumber discs, or pickled ginger.

INGREDIENTS :

1/4	cup marmalade
1/4	cup vinegar
1/4	tsp. salt

PREPARATION:

- Mix the ingredients in a pot, heat, stirring just long enough to mix together well, and then transfer to a bowl.
- Serves four.

Khanom Pang Na Mu

(Fried Canapés with Pork Spread)

INGREDIENTS :

1 1/2	cups ground pork
1	beaten egg
2	tbsp. water
1	tbsp. light soy sauce
1	tsp. finely chopped coriander root
1/2	tsp. pepper
5	cloves garlic
10	slices bread
1	finely sliced red chilli
4	cups cooking oil
1/4	cup chopped fresh coriander

PREPARATION:

■ Blend the pork with half of the egg. Pound the coriander root, pepper, and garlic well in a mortar and then knead into the pork mixture, adding the water.

■ Cut the slices of bread into quarters; these may be either square or triangular. Dry the bread by heating in a low temperature oven. Place about 1 tbsp. of the pork spread on each piece of bread and spread it so that it mounds in the center and slopes smoothly right to the edges. Smear the spread with some of the remaining egg and decorate with coriander greens and slices of red chilli.

■ Heat the oil in a wok. When it is hot, fry the pieces of bread spread-side downward until golden brown; then, remove from the oil and drain.

■ Serve with slices of fresh cucumber or with cucumber relish.

■ Serves four to six.

Mi Krop
(Crispy Candied Noodles)

INGREDIENTS :

5	oz. thin rice noodles
1/4	cup finely chopped fresh shrimp
1/4	cup finely chopped pork
1	cake yellow beancurd, cut into matchstick-size pieces and fried crisp
1	tbsp. chopped garlic and shallot
1	tbsp. fermented soybeans
1	tbsp. vinegar
1	tbsp. fish sauce
4	tbsp. palm sugar
1	tbsp. lime juice
1	tsp. ground dried chillies
2	oz. bean sprouts
3	Chinese chives (gao choy)
1	chilli, thinly sliced
1	coriander plant
2	pickled garlic bulbs, thinly sliced
3	cups cooking oil

PREPARATION:

■ If the noodles are very fine, fry in oil until crisp and golden brown, then drain. If the noodles are thick, soak **15** minutes in water, drain well, and then fry a few at a time.

■ Heat 1/4 cup oil in a frying pan. Fry the garlic and shallots until fragrant, then add the pork and shrimp, seasoning with fermented soybeans, vinegar, fish sauce, sugar and dried chilllies. When thick, add the lime juice. Mix and season to obtain a sweet, sour, and salty flavor.

■ Reduce the heat, add the noodles and continue stirring in the sauce until they stick together; then, add the beancurd; mix and spoon onto plates.

■ Sprinkle with the pickled garlic, finely sliced kaffir lime rind, coriander, and chilli. Place bean sprouts and Chinese chives along the sides of the plates.

■ Serves four.

Khao Tang Na Tang
(Fried Potcrust and Dip)

INGREDIENTS FOR FRIED POTCRUST :

1	lb. rice-pot crust
4	cups cooking oil

PREPARATION:

■ Place the oil in a deep wok over medium heat. When the oil is hot, fry the potcrust a few pieces at a time, turning as necessary until golden brown on both sides; then, remove from the oil and drain.

bread can also be fried crisp in this way.

INGREDIENTS FOR DIP :

1/2	cup minced pork
1/2	cup minced prawn (about 7 oz. fresh prawns)
1/4	cup ground roasted peanuts
1 3/4	cups coconut milk
1	dried chilli, seeds removed and soaked in water
1	tsp. sliced coriander root
1/4	tsp. pepper
4	cloves garlic
2	tbsp. sugar
1-2	tbsp. fish sauce
1	tbsp. thinly sliced shallot
1	tbsp. chopped fresh corainder

PREPARATION:

■ Pound the coriander root, pepper, chilli, and garlic well in a mortar.

■ Bring the coconut milk to a boil in a wok. When some oil has surfaced, add the coriander root-pepper-garlic mixture and stir to disperse. Next, add the prawns and pork, stir well and season to taste with the sugar and fish sauce. When the dip has come to a boil once again, add the peanuts and shallots, remove from heat, and sprinkle with a little chopped fresh coriander.

■ Serve with fried potcrust, crisp fried bread, or melba toast.

■ Serves three to four.

Nam Phrik Ong

(Pork and Tomato Chilli Dip)

INGREDIENTS :

5	dried chillies, soaked
1	tbsp. finely sliced galangal
3	tbsp. chopped onion
5	cloves garlic (whole)
1	tsp. salt
1	tsp. shrimp paste
3	tbsp. chopped pork
1	cup cherry tomatoes
3	cloves garlic, chopped
1	coriander plant
2	tbsp. cooking oil
1/2	cup water

Fresh Vegetables :
cucumber, yard-long beans, winged beans
Boiled Vegetables :
yard-long beans, eggplant, pumpkin vine tips,
swamp cabbage, banana blossom

PREPARATION:

■ Pound the chillies, salt, and galangal well in a mortar. Add the onion, shrimp paste, and the five garlic cloves and pound to mix thoroughly. Add the pork and continue pounding to mix. Finally, add the tomatoes and pound to mix well.

■ Heat the oil in a wok. When it is hot, add the chopped garlic. When the garlic is fragrant, add the pork and tomato chili paste and continue frying over low heat stirring until the ingredients take on a gloss; then, add the water.

■ Continue cooking with regular stirring until much of the water evaporates and the mixture becomes fairly thick. Then, transfer to a bowl, sprinkle with chopped coriander, and serve with fresh vegetables, boiled vegetables or both.

■ Serves four.

Lon Tao Jiao

(Coconut Milk and Fermented Soybean Dip)

INGREDIENTS :

1	lb. grated coconut or 1 1/2 cups coconut milk
1/2	cup fermented soybean
3	tbsp. chopped shrimp
3	tbsp. chopped pork
4	shallots
3-5	chillies
3	tbsp. sugar
3	tbsp. tamarind juice

PREPARATION:

■ Add 3/4 cup warm water to the coconut and squeeze out 1 1/2 cups coconut milk.

■ Heat the coconut milk in wok until oil comes to the surface.

■ Strain the fermented soybean, place the solids in a mortar with 2 shallots and pound until mixed thoroughly. Mix with coconut milk in the wok over low heat. Add the shrimp, pork, and chillies and cook over low heat until done. Add 2 sliced shallots, sugar and tamarine juice to taste, bring to a boil and remove from heat.

■ Serve with fresh vegetables, such as cabbage, cucumbers, and coriander.

■ Serves four.

Kalampli Phan Tao Hu
(Stuffed Cabbage)

INGREDIENTS :

8	good-sized cabbage leaves
1	tsp. salt
2	Chinese celery plants or 8 cocktail toothpicks (see page 20)
3	cakes soft white bean curd
1/4	cup finely chopped garlic plant
1/2	lb. ground pork
2 1/2	tbsp. sugar
5	tbsp. ligth soy sauce
1	egg
2	cups chicken stock
1	tbsp. corn flour

thin slices of lime

PREPARATION:

■ Wash the cabbage leaves well, taking care not to tear them. Immerse the leaves in boiling water to which salt has been added. When the leaves have become flexible enough to be used for wrapping, remove from the water.

■ Wash the celery, remove the roots and leaves, and immerse the stalks in boiling water until flexible enough to be used for tying the cabbage leaves closed.

■ In a wok over low heat, fry the pork and garlic plant, breaking up the pork into small bits and adding 1/2 tbsp. sugar and 1 tbsp. light soy sauce. When the pork is done, add the bean curd, again breaking it up into small bits. Then, reduce the heat, add the egg, and stir to mix thoroughly.

■ Divide the filling into eight portions, placing each in the middle of a cabbage leaf. Fold two opposite sides over the filling, roll up tightly, and tie with celery stalks, or pin closed with toothpicks.

■ Arrange the stuffed cabbage leaves in wok, add the chicken stock and the remaining light soy sauce and sugar, and simmer for about 20 minutes.

■ Mix the corn flour with 2 tbsp. water to obtain a smooth batter, pour this into the wok, reduce the heat, and allow the sauce to thicken.

■ Arrange the stuffed cabbage leaves on a serving plate, pour the sauce over them, and place lime slices on top.

■ Serves four.

Kaeng Som Cha-Am
(Cha-Am Sour Tamarind Soup)

INGREDIENTS FOR SPICE MIXTURE :

3	small dried red chilies
1	tsp. salt
1 1/2	tsp. chopped fresh lemon grass
2	medium-sized shallots
1	tsp. shrimp paste

OTHER INGREDEINTS :

1 1/2	lbs. medium-sized prawns shelled and deveined or sea perch
2	lbs. fresh green vegetables (e.g., yard-long beans, cabbage, cauliflower, Chinese cabbage)
4 1/2	cups chicken stock or water
4	tbsp. fish sauce
2	tbsp. sugar
5	tbsp. tamarind juice

PREPARATION:

■ Into a blender put the dried chillies, salt, lemon grass, shallots, shrimp paste and a little of the chicken stock and blend well.

■ Into a pot pour the remaining chicken stock, add the blended ingredients, and heat to a boil. Next, add sugar, fish sauce and tamarind juice to taste. If not sour enough, add more tamarind juice.

■ Then, add the prawns or the fish and the vegetables. Do not overcook.

■ Serve hot.

■ Serves six.

Tom Yam Kung
(Sour and Spicy Prawn Soup)

INGREDIENTS :

6	large prawns
3	cups chicken stock
5-6	hot chilles, just broken with pestle
2-3	kaffir lime leaves, torn
5	slices galangal
1	lemon grass stem, cut into short sections
2	coriander plants, chopped coarsely
4	tbsp. lime juice
3	tbsp. fish sauce
1/2	lb. mushrooms, halved

PREPARATION:

■ Shell and devein the prawns; then, wash them thoroughly.

■ Heat the stock to boiling. Add the lemon grass, galangal, and prawns; season to taste with lime juice, chillies, and fish sauce. Add kaffir lime leaves, chopped coriander and mushrooms. Remove from the heat, and serve hot.

Instead of chillies, 1 tsp. ground pepper may be mixed with the stock.

■ Serves four.

Tom Yam Kai
(Sour and Spicy Chicken Soup)

INGREDIENTS :

1	lb. boneless chicken meat, diced
3	cups chicken stock
5-6	hot chillies, just broken with pestle
2-3	kaffir lime leaves, torn
6	cherry tomatoes
1	lemon grass stem
4	tbsp. lime juice
3	tbsp. fish sauce
1/2	lb. straw mushrooms, halved
1/2	tsp. sugar

PREPARATION:

■ Cut the lemon grass into 1-inch lengths. Place the stock in a pot, add the lemon grass and kaffir lime leaves, and bring to a boil over medium heat. Add the chicken meat, fish sauce, lime juice and sugar; cook slowly and uncovered for 10 minutes. Do not stir. Then add the tomatoes, mushrooms and chillies and cook for 5 more minutes. Remove from heat.

■ Serves four.

Tom Kha Kai

(Coconut Milk Chicken Soup)

INGREDIENTS :

3 1/2	cups coconut milk
1	lb. chicken (skinned, deboned and diced)
1/2	lb. fresh mushrooms, halved
1	oz. fresh galangal, sliced
1	oz. fresh lemon grass, cut into 1″ lengths
4-5	kaffir lime leaves, torn in half
2-3	fresh chillies, halved
1/3	cup lime juice
3	tbsp. fish sauce
3	tsp. sugar
1	tsp. salt
2	tbsp. chopped coriander greens
1	tbsp. roasted chilli sauce (nam phrik phao) **(see page 23)**

PREPARATION:

■ Put coconut milk into a medium-sized pot, add **1 cup water** and bring to a boil over medium heat. Reduce heat, add the galangal, lemon grass, kaffir lime leaves and cook for a few more minutes, stirring occasionally. Next, add the chicken, salt, fish sauce, sugar and lime juice, cook until the chicken is done. Then, add the mushrooms and remove from heat.

■ To Serve: Put 1 tbsp. of roasted chilli sauce in the bottom of a large serving bowl. Pour in the boiling soup.

■ Serves four.

Kaeng Liang Ruam Phak
(Fish-Flavored Vegetable Soup)

INGREDIENTS FOR SPICE MIXTURE :

10	pepper corns
1	tbsp. shrimp paste
10	shallots
1/2	cup dried shrimp or fish

OTHER INGREDIENTS :

5	cups (18 oz.) sponge gourd, bottle-gourd, or other gourd, and baby corn
5	stems of sweet basil (maenglak)
4	cups soup stock or water
2-3	tbsp. fish sauce

PREPARATION:

■ Place spice mixture ingredients in a mortar and pound until mixed thoroughly.

■ Add spice mixture to soup stock (or water) in a pot and heat to boiling, stirring to prevent sticking. Do not cover the pot or allow to boil over.

■ Wash the vegetables. If gourd is used, peel and cut into 1/2 inch strips. Other vegetables are separated into individual leaves.

■ When the water boils, add fish sauce, or, if the odor of this is offensive, salt may be substituted. Add the vegetables and boil. When vegetables are done, season to taste with fish sauce or salt, as desired; then, remove from heat.

■ Serves four.

Kaeng Joet Wun Sen

(Mungbean Noodle Soup)

INGREDIENTS :

1	cup mungbean noodles, soaked and cut into short lengths
2	oz. ear mushroom or champignon
1	cup chopped or finely sliced pork
5	small prawns
1	tsp. finely sliced coriander root
1/4	tsp. pepper
5	cloves garlic
2	spring onions
3 1/2	cups soup stock
3	tbsp. fish sauce or light soy sauce
2	tbsp. cooking oil

PREPARATION:

■ Pound the coriander root, pepper, and garlic well in a mortar.

■ Heat the oil in a wok. When hot, fry the garlic mixture until fragrant. Add the pork, prawns and some fish sauce, along with 1/2 cup of the stock, the noodles, and the mushrooms.

■ Continue frying for about 5 minutes and then transfer the contents of the wok to a pot, add the remaining soup stock, heat to boiling, and add fish sauce to taste. Remove from the heat, garnish with spring onions and serve.

■ Serves four.

Lap Mu
(Savory Chopped-Pork Salad)

INGREDIENTS :

2	cups ground lean pork
4	oz. pork liver
5-6	tbsp. lime juice
2	tbsp. ground pan-roasted rice or dry breadcrumbs
1/2	tsp. ground chilli
2	tbsp. fish sauce
2	coriander plants, chopped
2	spring onions, sliced
1/2	cup mint leaves
1	tbsp. thinly sliced shallot

PREPARATION:

■ Mix the pork with 4 tbsp. lime juice and work with squeezing movements of the hand; then, squeeze the pork to drive out excess liquid. Now, immerse the pork in boiling water, stir, and remove from the water when done.

■ Boil the liver until done and then cut into small, thin slices.

■ Mix the pork, liver, pan-roasted rice (or breadcrumbs), ground chilli, shallots, spring onions and coriander greens; season to taste with the fish sauce and the remaining lime juice. Sprinkle with mint leaves and serve with lettuce, cabbage, and yard-long beans.

■ Serves four.

Lap Kai

(Savory Chopped-Chicken Salad)

INGREDIENTS :

3	cups coarsely chopped chicken
5	thinly sliced shallots
3	sliced spring onions
1/4	cup lime juice
1	tsp. salt
1/2	tsp. ground chilli
2	tbsp. ground pan-roasted rice or dry breadcrumbs
1/4	cup coarsely chopped coriander greens
1/4	cup mint leaves

PREPARATION:

■ Mix the chicken and the salt, place in a covered baking dish, and bake at 400°F. for about ten minutes or until done. After removing from the oven and allowing to cool somewhat, knead to break up the mass of baked chicken.

■ Add the ground chilli, pan-roasted rice (or breadcrumbs), shallots, spring onions, and lime juice; toss gently. Add the mint leaves and corinader greens, toss once again, arrange upon a bed of lettuce, and serve with sliced cucumber, yard-long beans, and cabbage.

■ Serves four.

Neua Nam Tok
(Savory Beef Salad)

INGREDIENTS :

1	lb. beef cut into thin strips about 1 inch wide and 2 inches long
1	tbsp. thinly sliced lemon grass
1 1/2	tbsp. well-pounded parched rice
1/2	cup thinly sliced shallot
1/2	cup coarsely chopped mint leaves
4 1/2	tbsp. lime juice
3	tbsp. fish sauce
1/2	cup chopped coriander greens
1/2	tsp. ground dried chilli
1	tbsp. chopped spring onion
1/4	tsp. sugar
1	lettuce plant

PREPARATION:

■ Grill sliced beef strips to medium rare.

■ In a mixing bowl, mix all remaining ingredients well, add beef and toss well.

■ Serve the beef on a bed of lettuce with spring onions.

■ Serves three to four.

Yam Kai Yang

(Spicy Barbecued-Chicken Salad)

INGREDIENTS FOR SPICE SAUCE DRESSING :

1	tbs. ground chilli
2	tbsp. vinegar
2	tbsp. lime juice
1	tbsp. sugar
2	tbsp. fish sauce
1/2	tsp. salt

OTHER INGREDIENTS :

1	barbecued chicken
1	thinly sliced onion
1	thinly sliced tomato
1 1/2	tbsp. ground roasted peanuts
3-4	lettuce leaves

PREPARATION:

■ Make up the dressing by mixing all ingredients and then heating to a boil. Add the peanuts.

■ Separate the chicken into pieces and cut each piece diagonally into thin slices.

■ Pour the dressing onto the chicken and stir lightly. Add the onion and tomato, stir again.

■ Arrange the salad onto a bed of lettuce arranged on a platter, serve with fresh vegetables, such as cabbage.

■ Serves four to five.

Yam Pla Meuk

(Spicy Squid Salad)

INGREDIENTS FOR DRESSING :

2	tbsp. sliced garlic
2-3	hot chillies
1/4	cup lime juice
3-4	tbsp. fish sauce

PREPARATION:

■ Pound the chillies and garlic well in a mortar and mix with the lime juice and fish sauce.

INGREDIENTS :

1	lb. fresh squid
1	cup thinly sliced onion
1/4	cup thinly sliced young ginger
1	cup celery cut into 1-inch lengths
1	lettuce plant
1	coriander plant, root removed and coarsely chopped or mint leaves
1	red chilli, thinly sliced for use as garnish

PREPARATION:

■ Wash the squid, remove the bone, eyes, and the skin. Cut across the squid into about 1 cm.-thick rings or score (i.e., make shallow cuts with the knife on the outer surface of the squid in a criss-cross pattern). Then, cut the squid into 1 1/2 inch pieces.

■ Scald the squid in boiling water. Do not leave the squid in the water long, for it will become tough.

■ Gently toss the squid together with the onion, ginger, celery, and the dressing, and if necessary, season with additional fish sauce or lime juice.

■ Arrange lettuce leaves around the edge of a serving dish, place the squid salad in the middle, and sprinkle with red chilli and coriander or mint leaves.

■ Serves four.

Yam Sam Sahai

(Spicy Pork, Prawn, and Chicken Salad)

INGREDIENTS :

1 1/2	cups sliced steamed pork
1 1/2	cups sliced steamed chicken
1 1/2	cups sliced steamed prawns
	(In each case, the slices should be cut
	on a diagonal to the grain of the meat.)
3	tbsp. roasted chilli sauce(nam phrik phao) **(See page 23)**
3	tbsp. fish sauce
1/4	cup lime juice
1	tsp. sugar
2-3	tbsp. tamarind juice
1/4	cup roasted peanuts or cashew nuts, broken
	into chunks
1	Chinese radish
1	carrot
1/2	cup chopped celery
1/2	cup mint leaves
2	head romain lettuce
1/2	head cabbage
5	spring onions

PREPARATION:

■ Make the sauce by mixing the roasted chilli sauce, fish sauce, sugar, and tamarind juice in a pot and heating to a boil. Allow to boil a few moments; then, remove from the heat, add the lime juice, and stir.

■ When the sauce has cooled, add the pork, chicken, prawn, and celery, mix thoroughly, and then add the mint. Scoop onto a bed of lettuce prepared on a serving platter, sprinkle with the peanuts or cashews, and serve with spring onions, cabbage, and thin slices of carrot and Chinese radish.

■ Serves four.

Phla Mu Op
(Savory Baked Pork Salad)

INGREDIENTS :

1	lb. pork
5	lemon grass stems. Take only the swollen base of the stem, where it is tinged with purple and slice thin.
10	thinly sliced shallots
7	kaffir lime leaves, sliced into thin strips
3	tbsp. chopped coriander greens
3	tbsp. thinly sliced spring onion
1/2	cup mint leaves
10	hot chillies
15	cloves garlic
1/2	tsp. salt
4	tbsp. lime juice
1	tbsp. whiskey
1	tbsp. ground black pepper
fish sauce	
sugar	

PREPARATION:

■ Pound the chillies and garlic together with the salt well in a mortar and then add the lime juice and enough sugar and fish sauce to give the dressing a pleasing flavor.

■ Cut the pork into 1-inch pieces, add a little maggi sauce, whiskey, pepper, and sugar, place in an oven-proof dish, and bake at 450°F. for 10 minutes.

■ Place the pork on a serving dish, add the prepared lemon grass, shallots, kaffir lime leaves, coriander greens, and spring onions, pour on the dressing. Toss well, and serve immediately.

■ Serves four.

Yam Wun Sen
(Spicy Mungbean Noodle Salad)

INGREDIENTS FOR DRESSING :

1	tbsp. thinly sliced coriander root
1	thinly sliced bulb of pickled garlic
1	thinly sliced chilli
1/3	cup vinegar
1/3	cup sugar
1	tsp. salt

PREPARATION:

■ Pound the coriander root, pickled garlic, and chilli well in a mortar. Place this mixture in a pot, add the vinegar, sugar, and salt, and heat. When the mixture comes to a boil, remove from the heat and allow to cool.

INGREDIENTS FOR SALAD :

2	cups short lengths of scalded mungbean noodles
1/2	cup thin slices of boiled pork
1/2	cup thin slices of boiled pork liver
1/2	cup thin slices of boiled prawn
1/2	cup thinly sliced onion
1	cup 1-inch lengths of celery
1	tomato cut into thin wedges
1	lettuce plant
1/4	cup crisp fried dried shrimp

PREPARATION:

■ Mix the noodles, pork, liver, prawns, onions, and celery. Add the dressing and toss gently; then, add the tomato.

■ Place the salad on a bed of lettuce and sprinkle with the fried dried shrimp.

■ Serves four.

Phla Kung

(Savory Prawn Salad)

INGREDIENTS :

10	oz. prawns
5	hot chillies
2	stems lemon grass
3	shallots
20	mint leaves
1	coriander plant
1	tbsp. shredded kaffir lime leaves
1	tbsp. lime juice
1	tbsp. fish sauce

PREPARATION:

■ Wash, shell, and devein the prawns. Immerse for a short time in boiling water; the prawns should be not quite done.

■ Slice the chillies, lemon grass, and shallots thin.

■ Pick the leaves from the coriander plant. Wash them and the mint leaves and then drain.

■ Toss the prawns with the lime juice and fish sauce. Add the lemon grass, chillies, shallots, and kaffir lime leaves and toss to mix. The flavor should be spicy.

■ Transfer to a serving dish and garnish with coriander and mint leaves.

■ Serves two to three.

Naem Sot
(Piquant Chopped Pork Salad)

INGREDIENTS :

1	cup finely chopped pork
1/2	cup finely sliced boiled pig skin
1	tsp. salt
1	tbsp. sliced garlic
3-4	tbsp. lime juice
1/4	cup finely sliced young ginger root
1/4	cup sliced onions
1/4	cup chopped coriander and spring onions
1/2	cup roasted peanuts
1	head romaine lettuce
1-2	tbsp. fried dried chillies

PREPARATION:

■ Mix the salt with the pork; then, dry fry over low heat until done, breaking the meat into small fragments. Remove from heat, allow to cool, add the pig skin and mix thoroughly.

■ Gently blend in garlic, salt, lime juice, ginger, and onion and season to taste.

■ Spoon the mixture onto a bed of lettuce. Sprinkle with coriander and spring onions. Serve with roasted peanuts, fried dried chillies, lettuce and other vegetables.

■ Serves two to three.

Yam Thua Phu
(Spicy Winged-Bean Salad)

INGREDIENTS :

1/2	lb. winged beans
1/2	cup steamed pork sliced into small pieces
1/4	cup coconut milk
2	tbsp. fried sliced shallot
2	tbsp. coarsely ground roasted peanuts
2	tbsp. fish sauce
1 1/2	tbsp. sugar
2	tbsp. lime juice
1	small pan-roasted dried chilli
2	small roasted shallots
1	small roasted garlic bulb

PREPARATION:

■ Immerse the winged beans in boiling water for 3 minutes and then cut into small pieces.

■ Bring the coconut milk to a boil and then remove from the heat.

■ Pound the chilli, the roasted shallots, and the garlic well in a mortar; then, add the sugar, fish sauce, and lime juice, mix thoroughly and transfer to a bowl.

■ Add the winged beans, pork, boiled coconut milk, fried shallot, and peanut, toss to mix well, and then place on a serving platter.

■ Serves two to three.

Salat Khaek
(Southern Thai Salad)

INGREDIENTS FOR DRESSING :

2	dried chillies, seeds removed and soaked in water
1/4	tsp. salt
1/4	cup thinly sliced shallot
1	tsp. curry powder
2	hard-boiled eggs
1/2	cup ground roasted peanuts
2	cups coconut milk
3	tbsp. fish sauce
1/3	cup sugar
1/4	cup tamarind juice

PREPARATION:

■ Pound the chillies, salt, shallots, and curry powder well in a mortar and then mix in the peanuts. Remove the yolks from the two eggs and mix the yolks into the chilli paste.

■ Heat 1 cup of the coconut milk. When some oil has surfaced, add the chilli paste, stir to disperse, and cook until fragrant; then, add the remaining coconut milk, fish sauce, sugar, and tamarind juice.

INGREDIENTS FOR SALAD :

1	potato
3	hard-boiled eggs cuts into slices
1	cake firm white beancurd
1	head romaine lettuce
1	cup scalded beansprouts
5	cucumbers (see page 20)
1	onion
2	tomatoes
2	cups cooking oil

PREPARATION:

■ Cut the potato into very thin slices, soak in water, drain well, and then fry in the hot oil until crisp and golden brown. Cut the beancurd into thin slices and fry in the oil until crisp.

■ Peel the cucumbers and onion and cut them and the tomatoes into thin slices.

■ Arrange the lettuce on a platter, add the cucmbers, bean sprouts, onion, tomatoes, eggs, beancurd, and potato, spoon on the salad dressing, and serve right away.

■ Serves two.

Som Tam Malako
(Papaya Salad)

INGREDIENTS :

1	peeled and shredded green papaya (about 4 cups)
6	garlic cloves
1	dried chilli soaked in water
7	pepper corns
1	tbsp. tamarind juice
3	tbsp. fish sauce
3	tbsp. palm sugar
2	tbsp. lime juice
1/4	cup ground dried shrimp
1/4	cup lime cut into small cubes

cabbage, lettuce and leaves of chaphlu and various sliced vegetables

PREPARATION:

- Gently crush the shredded papaya in a mortar with a pestle. Remove and set aside.
- Crush the garlic, dried chilli, and pepper corns in mortar, mixing thoroughly.
- Mix the tamarind juice, fish sauce, and sugar in a pot and heat to a boil. Remove from heat, allow to cool, add lime juice, and mix in the chilli mixture
- Add the crushed papaya, the dried shrimp and the lime cubes and mix thoroughly.
- Serve with lettuce and other sliced vegetables of choice.
- Serves four.

Kung Phat Som Makham Piak
(Stir-Fried Prawns in Tamarind Sauce)

INGREDIENTS :

1	lb. jumbo prawns shelled and deveined
2	tbsp. chicken broth or water
1	tsp. salt
1/3	cup tamarind juice
7	fried, dried red chillies
2	tbsp. chopped onion
1	tbsp. fish sauce
1	tbsp. fried minced garlic
2	tbsp. fried sliced shallot
2	tbsp. palm sugar
1/3	cup chopped spring onion
1	red bell pepper thinly sliced
1/4	cup chopped coriander
2	tbsp. vegetable oil

PREPARATION:

■ Put the vegetable oil in a wok over medium heat. Brown the onion; add the palm sugar, chicken broth, salt, tamarind juice, fish sauce and chillies, stirring and turning with a spatula.

■ When the liquid begins to boil, add the prawns, garlic, shallots and spring onions, and remove when prawns are done.

■ Garnish with coriander and red bell pepper.

■ Serves two to three.

Kung Kra Thiam

(Garlic Prawn)

INGREDIENTS :

8-12	jumbo prawns, shelled and deveined
2	tbsp. chopped garlic
1	tsp. pepper
1/2	tbsp. fish sauce
1 1/4	tsp. sugar
1	tbsp. chopped coriander root
4	tbsp. vegetable oil
1/2	cup chopped spring onion
1/4	cup chopped or minced ginger

PREPARATION:

■ In a wok or big frying pan, heat the oil over high heat. Fry the garlic, coriander root, pepper, sugar, fish sauce and prawns, stirring constantly. Cook for 2 minutes and then add the remaining ingredients, stir well, and remove from heat.

■ Serves three to four.

Kung Yang Sot Makham Piak
(Broiled Lobster in Tamarind Sauce)

INGREDIENTS :

2	1 lb lobsters
2 1/2	tbsp. palm sugar
1 1/2	tbsp. fish sauce
1/2	tsp. salt
1	tbsp. chopped coriander root
1/3	cup thinly sliced shallot
1/3	cup chopped coriander greens
2 1/2	tbsp. tamarind juice
4-5	fried dried small red chillies
1 1/2	tbsp. vegetable oil
1	tbsp. finely chopped garlic
1	tbsp. water

PREPARATION:

■ Put the oil in a wok over medium heat. Fry the garlic, shallots and coriander root. When browned, remove from the wok and set aside.

■ Return the wok to the heat. In it, mix the palm sugar, tamarind juice, salt, chillies, fish sauce, and water. When the mixture comes to a boil, remove from the heat.

■ Broil the lobsters and then arrange on a serving platter. Sprinkle them with the fried garlic and shallots and then pour the sauce over them. Just before serving, sprinkle with chopped coriander.

■ Serves two.

Kaeng Ka-ri Kung
(Curried Prawns)

INGREDIENTS :

1 1/2	lb. prawns , shelled and deveined
2 1/2	cups coconut milk
1	tbsp. yellow curry paste (Nam Phrik Kaeng) Ka-ri, see p. 24)
2	fresh chillies, deseeded and sliced
1/2	cup cherry tomatoes
2	tbsp. fish sauce
1 1/2	tbsp. sugar
1	tsp. salt

PREPARATION:

- Put 3/4 cups of coconut milk into a wok or pan, bring to boil over medium heat, stirring constantly, and boil for 5 minutes.
- Add the curry paste, stir well, and simmer for 10 minutes.
- Then, add the fish sauce, sugar, salt and remaining coconut milk and simmer for 10 more minutes, stirring regularly.
- Finally, put in the chillies, tomatoes and prawns, bring to a boil, and remove from heat.
- Serve with cucumber relish. (See p. 37)
- Serves four.

Kaeng Matsaman Neua reu Kai reu Mu

(Beef, Chicken, or Pork Massaman Curry)

INGREDIENTS :

3	tbsp. matsaman curry paste (See p. 23)
1	lb. beef, chicken, or pork
1 1/2	lbs. grated coconut or 3 cups coconut milk
2	tbsp. roasted peanuts
5	peeled small onions (4 oz.)
5	small potatoes (4 oz.) peeled and boiled
3	bay leaves
5	roasted cardamom pods
1	piece of roasted cinnamon, 1 cm. long
3	tbsp. palm sugar
2	tbsp. fish sauce
3	tbsp. tamarind juice
3	tbsp. lemon juice

PREPARATION

■ Cut beef, chicken, or pork into 2 inch chunks.

■ Add 1 1/2 cups warm water to the coconut and squeeze out 3 cups coconut milk. Skim off 1 cup coconut cream to be used in cooking the curry paste. Place the remaining coconut milk in a pot with the chicken, pork, or beef and simmer until tender. (If beef is used, 2 additional cups of coconut milk will be needed because of the longer cooking time required.)

■ Heat the coconut cream in a wok until oil appears on surface; then, add the curry paste and cook until fragrant. Spoon this mixture into the pot containing the meat and add the peanuts. Taste and adjust the flavor so it is sweet, salty, and sour by adding sugar, fish sauce, tamarind juice, and lemon juice. Add bay leaves, cardamom, cinnamon, potatoes, and onions, simmer until tender.

■ Serve with pickled ginger or cucumber relish. (See p. 37)

■ Serves four.

Kaeng Phet Kai Sai No Mai
(Chicken in Red Curry with Bamboo Shoots)

INGREDIENTS :

1	lb. diced, boneless chicken
1	tbsp. red curry paste (See p. 26)
3/4	cup coconut milk
1/2	cup sweet basil leaves (horapha)
5	kaffir lime leaves, halved
1	fresh red chilli (sliced lengthwise into 8 pieces)
1/2	cup sliced zucchini
2	tbsp. fish sauce
1/4	tsp. salt
1/3	cup water
5	oz. bamboo shoots (sliced lengthwise)
1 1/2	tsp. sugar

PREPARATION:

■ In a pot, bring half the coconut milk to a slow boil, stirring constantly. Put in the red curry paste and chicken, stir well, and cook until done (about 5 minutes).

■ Add the remaining coconut milk, water, bamboo shoots, sugar and fish sauce, and bring slowly to a boil. Add salt to taste.

■ Add the zucchini, kaffir lime leaves, and sliced chilli; remove from heat. Garnish with sweet basil.

■ Serves four to five.

Ho Mok Mu reu Kai reu Pla
(Steamed Curried Pork, Chicken, or Fish)

INGREDIENTS FOR SPICE MIXTURE :

5	dried chillies, seeds removed and soaked in water
3	garlic bulbs
2	tbsp. finely sliced galangal
2	tbsp. finely sliced lemon grass
1	tsp. finely sliced kaffir-lime rind
2	tsp. finely sliced coriander root
5	pepper corns
1/2	tsp. salt
1	tsp. shrimp paste
1	tsp. finely sliced krachai (if fish is used)

OTHER INGREDIENTS :

1	lb. pork, chicken, or filleted fish
3	tbsp. fish sauce
1	egg
2	cups coconut milk
1	tsp. rice flour
2	cups sweet basil leaves (horapha)
2	tbsp. finely chopped coriander greens
1	finely sliced red chilli
3	tbsp. shredded kaffir-lime leaf

PREPARATION:

■ Pound the spice mixture ingredients well in a mortar.

■ Chop the pork but not too finely; if chicken is used, cut it into small pieces; if fish is used, cut the fillets into thin slices.

■ Skim 3/4 cup coconut cream from the coconut milk, add rice flour, bring to a boil, remove from the heat, and set aside for topping.

■ Stir 1 cup coconut milk with the pounded spice mixture, add the meat or fish, the egg, the fish sauce, and then the remaining coconut milk a little at a time. Add 1/2 cup basil leaves, 1 tbsp. coriander greens, and 2 tsp.. kaffir lime leaf and stir to mix in.

■ Place the remaining sweet basil leaves in the bottoms of custard cups, fill each cup with the mixture, and steam for 15 minutes. Remove the cups from the steamer, top each one with some of the boiled coconut cream and a little coriander greens, kaffir lime leaf, and sliced chilli, return to the steamer to steam for one minute, and then remove from the steamer.

■ Shredded cabbage may be substituted for sweet basil leaves.

■ Serves four.

Kaeng Phet Het

(Red Curry of Mushrooms)

INGREDIENTS :

1/2	cup sweet basil leaves (horapha)
1/2	lb. fresh mushrooms (halved)
1	tbsp. red curry paste (See p. 26)
1/2	tbsp. sugar
3	tbsp. fish sauce
1	tsp. chopped kaffir lime leaf
1	sliced whole medium red or green chilli
1 1/2	cups coconut milk
1/2	cup water (or chicken stock)

PREPARATION:

- Put half of the coconut milk in a wok over medium heat. Add the red curry paste and stir until thoroughly mixed.
- Add the remaining coconut milk, chicken stock, mushrooms, fish sauce, sugar, kaffir lime leaves, chilli and basil.
- Do not overcook mushrooms.
- Serves three to four.

Kaeng Khiao Wan Neua
(Thai Beef Curry)

INGREDIENTS :

3	tbsp. green curry paste (See P. 25)
1	lb. beef
1	lb. grated coconut or 2 1/2 cups coconut milk
4	oz. eggplant (makheua phuang)
2	kaffir lime leaves
1/4	cup sweet basil leaves (horapha)
1 1/2-2	tbsp. fish sauce
1	tbsp. palm sugar
1	tbsp. cooking oil

PREPARATION:

■ Cut beef into long, thin slices.

■ Add 2 cups warm water to the coconut and squeeze out 1 cup coconut cream and 1 1/2 cups coconut milk.

■ Fry the curry paste in oil until fragrant, reduce heat, add the coconut cream a little at a time, stirring until the coconut cream begins to have an oily sheen.

■ Add the beef and torn kaffir lime leaves and cook a short time; then, pour the curry into a pot, add the coconut milk and sugar. Add fish sauce to taste, and heat. When boiling, add the eggplant. When the meat is done, add the sweet basil and remove from heat.

■ Pork or chicken can be used in place of beef.

■ Serves four.

Kai Kolae
(Southern-Thai-Style Braised Chicken)

SPICE MIXTURE INGREDIENTS :

5	dried chillies, seeds removed and soaked in water
1	tsp. salt
1/4	tsp. ground roasted coriander seeds
1/4	tsp. ground roasted cumin seeds
1/4	tsp. ground cinnamon
2	tbsp. thinly sliced shallots
1	tbsp. chopped garlic
1	tsp. chopped fresh turmeric or curry powder
1	tsp. shrimp paste

OTHER INGREDIENTS :

1	young chicken weighing about 3 1/2 lbs.
5	cups coconut milk
4	tbsp. butter
2	tbsp. cooking oil
3	tbsp. fish sauce
2	tbsp. palm sugar
3	tbsp. lime juice

PREPARATION:

■ Pound the chillies and salt in a mortar. Add the garlic and shallots and pound well; then, add the turmeric (or curry powder) and pound fine. Add the coriander, cumin, and cinnamon and pound to mix well. Finally, add the shrimp paste and mix in thoroughly.

■ Clean the chicken, cut into 10-12 pieces, and fry in the butter and cooking oil. When the chicken is golden brown, transfer it to a pot, add the coconut milk, and place on a medium heat. When the coconut milk comes to a boil, reduce the heat and simmer for 30 minutes.

■ Place the butter and oil remaining from the frying of the chicken in a wok on a medium heat, and fry the spice mixture. When fragrant, add to the pot and season with fish sauce, lime juice, and palm sugar.

■ When the chicken is tender, arrange on a serving platter, garnish with red chillies, and serve with steamed rice.

■ Serves four to five.

Pha-naeng Neua
(Beef Curried in Sweet Peanut Sauce)

INGREDIENTS :

1	lb. beef, cut into thin strips
3	tbsp. pha-naeng curry paste (or red curry paste) (See p. 26)
6	fresh or dry kaffir lime leaves (halved)
1/2	cup sweet basil leaves (horapha)
1	fresh chilli (seeded and cut into strips)
2	cups coconut milk
1/3	cup chicken stock
3	tbsp. palm sugar
2 1/2	tbsp. fish sauce
1/4	tsp. salt
1/2	cup ground roasted peanuts

PREPARATION:

■ Put the coconut milk into medium-sized sauce pan over medium heat, add the curry paste and slowly bring to a boil, stirring constantly.

■ Put in beef strips and cook for 5 minutes.

■ Meanwhile, in a bowl, mix the rest of the ingredients except for the sweet basil and fresh chilli. Add this to the curried beef, and simmer about 15 minutes. Add the sweet basil and fresh chilli, stir well, and remove from the heat.

■ Serves four to five.

Pik Kai Sot Sai Pha-naeng
(Stuffed Chicken Wings in Pha-naeng Sauce)

INGREDIENTS

3	tbsp. red curry paste (See p. 26)
12	chicken wings
1	cup chopped chicken breast
4	cups coconut milk
3	tbsp. fish sauce
2	tbsp. palm sugar
2	tbsp. shredded kaffir lime leaf
1/2	cup sweet basil leaves (horapha)
1	tbsp. thinly sliced chilli

PREPARATION:

■ Slit open the wings, remove the bones, being careful not to tear the skin, and cut off the pointed tip of each wing (see p. 26).

■ Blend the chicken breast with 1 tbsp. of the curry paste and 1 tbsp. fish sauce.

■ Put some of the stuffing into each wing but do not pack too tightly.

■ Close the slit by pinning the skin on either side together with a sliver of bamboo and shape so they look like chicken wings. Then, place the wings in a steamer and steam until done; 15 minutes.

■ Place 1 cup of coconut milk in a wok over medium heat. When some oil has surfaced, add the remaining curry paste and stir to disperse. When fragrant, add the remaining coconut milk a little at a time and season with fish sauce and sugar. Now, add the steamed chicken wings and season as necessary. Transfer the wings and sauce to a pot, close the lid, and simmer over a very low heat until the wings are tender and the liquid is much reduced in volume.

■ Place the wings on a serving dish and garnish with the kaffir lime leaf, chilli, sweet basil leaves, and coriander greens.

■ Serves four to six.

Kaeng Chuchi Pla
(Fish Curry)

INGREDIENTS :

3	tbsp. red curry paste (See p. 26)
1	lb. mackerel or other meaty fish
3	cups coconut milk
3	tbsp. fish sauce
2	tbsp. palm sugar
2	kaffir lime leaves cut into thin strips

PREPARATION:

■ Wash and clean the fish, remove the head, and score diagonally on both sides.

■ Deep fry the fish in hot oil until golden brown. Remove from oil and drain. Set aside.

■ Heat 1 cup coconut milk in a wok until some of the oil surfaces, add the curry paste and cook, stirring until dispersed and fragrant; then, add the rest of the coconut milk, when it comes to a boil, add the fish. Cook for two minutes moving the fish around gently.

■ Season to taste with fish sauce and palm sugar. Remove from heat.

■ Arrange on a serving plate and garnish with shreds of kaffir lime leaf.

Kaeng Phet Pet Yang

(Red Curry of Duck)

INGREDIENTS :

1	roasted duck, deboned and cut into 1 ″ squares
2 1/2	cups coconut milk
1 1/2	tbsp. vegetable oil
3	tbsp. red curry paste (See p. 26)
2	medium tomatoes, halved or 10 cherry tomatoes
1/2	cup sweet basil leaves (horapha)
4	kaffir lime leaves, halved
1/2	tsp. salt
2	tbsp. fish sauce
1	tsp. sugar
1/2	cup water (or chicken stock)

PREPARATION:

■ Put vegetable oil into wok over medium heat and add the red curry paste, stir well, add 3/4 cups coconut milk and stir to mix thoroughly.

■ Add the duck and stir well. Next, add the remaining coconut milk, water, tomatoes, kaffir lime leaves, sugar, salt, fish sauce and sweet basil.

■ Cook for about 10 minutes or until duck absorbs curry flavor.

■ Serves six.

Kaeng Khua Fak Kap Kai
(Chicken and Wax Gourd Curry)

INGREDIENTS :

3	tbsp. kaeng khua curry paste (See p. 24)
1	lb. chicken
1	lb. grated coconut or 3 cups coconut milk
1	lb. wax gourd
1	tbsp. tamarind juice
3	tbsp. palm sugar
3	tbsp. fish sauce

PREPARATION:

■ Clean the chicken, cut into 1 inch pieces.

■ Peel the gourd, remove the seeds, and cut it into 1 inch chunks.

■ Add 1 1/2 cups warm water to the coconut and squeeze out 3 cups coconut milk.

■ Skim off 1 cup coconut cream, place in a wok and heat. When oil begins to appear on the surface, add the spice mixture and stir in, then add the chicken and cook. Spoon into a pot, add the remaining coconut milk and the wax gourd and heat. When the gourd is done, season to taste with tamarind juice, palm sugar, and fish sauce.

■ Serves four.

Pla Kao Rat Sot Ma-kheua Thet
(Rock Cod Baked in Banana Leaf)

INGREDIENTS :

1	whole banana leaf (or foil)
1	medium-sized whole rock cod
1	cup tender Chinese kale
1/2	cup chopped canned pineapple
1	onion, sliced
1	large tomato, sliced
2	bell peppers, sliced
1/2	cup tomato sauce
1 1/2	tbsp. fish sauce
1	tbsp. dry white wine
1	tsp. sugar
1	tsp. pepper
1	tbsp. butter

PREPARATION:

■ Lightly butter an 8 by 10 inch piece of banana leaf (or foil). Put cleaned and scaled fish onto the center of the leaf. Pour tomato sauce and wine, along with the fish sauce and all remaining ingredients, over the fish. Wrap the fish, sealing it in the leaf, tie if necessary, and bake in an oven heated to 350°F. for 15-20 minutes.

■ Serves two to three.

Pla Kaphong Khao Neung Phrik Sot Manao
(Sea Perch Steamed with Chillies in Lime Sauce)

INGREDIENTS :

1	sea perch weighing about 18 oz.
6	peeled cloves of giant garlic
5	hot chillies
3	tbsp. lime juice
2	spring onions
1	cup chicken stock
1 1/2	tbsp. light soy sauce

PREPARATION:

■ Scale, clean, and wash the fish. With a knife, score the flesh along the length of the fish; then, place it in a deep bowl.

■ Chop the chillies and mix them with the chicken stock, lime juice, and soy sauce. The dominant taste should be sour.

■ Pour the mixture over the fish and place the spring onions cut into 1 inch lengths and the garlic alongside.

■ After the water has begun boiling, place the fish in a steamer and steam over high heat for about 15 minutes. Remove from the steamer and serve hot.

■ Serves two to three.

Kung Phao
(Charcoal-Broiled Lobster with Savory Sauce)

INGREDIENTS :

4	medium-sized lobsters
1 1/2	tbsp. chopped garlic
1	tbsp. sugar
1/2	tsp. salt
1/3	cup hot water
1/2	tbsp. chopped chillies
1	tsp. chopped fresh coriander
2	tbsp. lime juice

banana leaf (or foil)

PREPARATION:

■ Clean the lobsters, wrap each in banana leaf, and tie well. Grill over a charcoal fire about 12 minutes. Serve with the sauce.

■ Heat the sugar and water in a sauce pan over low heat, stirring until the sugar is dissolved. Turn off the heat, add the salt and stir well. Remove from heat and allow to cool; then, add the rest of the ingredients and mix thoroughly.

■ Serves four.

Khai Tun
(Beaten Egg Steamed with Pork)

INGREDIENTS :

2	eggs
3	tbsp. ground pork
2	tbsp. thinly sliced shallot
1/4	tsp. pepper
2	tbsp. light soy sauce
1	cup chicken stock
1	tbsp. chopped spring onion
1/4	tsp. salt
3	prawns, shelled and deveined

PREPARATION:

■ Beat the eggs in a mixing bowl, add the shallots, the stock, the pepper, light soy sauce and salt, stirring with a fork.

■ Divide the mixture into 3 portions. Put each portion into a small glass bowl.

■ Wrap each prawn with 1/3 of the pork.

■ After the water has begun boiling, place the cups in a steamer and steam until the egg mixture begins to cook. Place a prawn on top of the mixture in each cup. Continue steaming until the pork and prawns are done; about 10-15 minutes.

■ Remove the cups from the steamer and sprinkle with chopped spring onion. Serve hot.

■ Serves three.

Pu Ja
(Stuffed Crab)

INGREDIENTS :

3	meaty crabs
1	cup ground pork
2	eggs
1/2	tbsp. minced coriander root
1	tsp. minced garlic
1/4	tsp. pepper
1	tbsp. light soy sauce
1/2	tsp. salt
3	tbsp. fine breadcrumbs
2	cups cooking oil

coriander leaves and red spur chilli

PREPARATION:

■ Wash the crabs and then steam them whole. When done, remove all the meat, saving the shells for stuffing.

■ Knead together the crabmeat, pork, coriander root, garlic, pepper, soy sauce, salt, and one egg. When well mixed, pack this filling into crab shells.

■ Pour the oil into a frying pan and place on medium heat.

■ Beat the remaining egg well, add the beaten egg onto the exposed surface of the filling, and then sprinkle with breadcrumbs.

■ When the oil is hot, put the crabs into it with the exposed surface of the filling downward. When the surface of the filling turns golden brown, lift the crabs from the oil, drain, garnish with coriander leaves and chilli shreds, and serve with chilli sauce.

■ If crabmeat is bought ready steamed and without shells, pack the filling into small over-proof cups and add the beaten egg onto the exposed surface of the filling, and then sprinkle with breadcrumb. Bake at 350° F for 15 minutes or until golden brown. Then remove from the oven and allow to cool down before taking the filling out of the cups to serve.

■ Serves four.

Pla Meuk Yat Sai

(Sautéed Stuffed Squid)

INGREDIENTS :

6-8	medium-sized fresh whole squid
1/2	lb. ground pork
1	tsp. chopped coriander
1/4	tsp. pepper
1	tbsp. chopped garlic
1	tsp. fish sauce
1	tsp. sugar
1	tbsp. light soy sauce
1	egg (slightly beaten)
1	tsp. chopped onion

PREPARATIONS:

■ Clean the squid and set aside. In a bowl, mix the rest of the above ingredients by hand. Stuff this filling into the whole squid and steam for 15 minutes. Then, cut diagonally into slices.

■ Into the 1/4 cup of hot vegetable oil, add the sliced stuffed squid along with the remaining ingredients listed below and fry for 5 minutes. Drain and serve with steamed rice.

2	tsp. sliced fresh ginger
1/2	cup spring onion cut in 1″ lengths
1/2	cup sliced Shiitake mushroom
1	tbsp. oyster sauce
1/4	cup oil
1	tsp. minced garlic

■ Serves six.

Pla Jalamet Khao Thot
(Fried White Pompano)

INGREDIENTS :

1	white pompano weighing about 1 lb.
1	tbsp. tapioca flour
3-4	thinly sliced hot chillies
1-2	thinly sliced shallots
1	tsp. lime juice
2	tbsp. fish sauce
3	cups cooking oil

PREPARATION:

■ Clean and wash the fish. With a knife, score both sides of the fish attractively. Then, turn the fish in the flour to coat on all sides.

■ Place the oil in a frying pan on medium heat. When the oil is hot, fry the fish until golden brown. Remove the fish from the pan and drain.

■ Serve with a sauce made by mixing the shallots, chilli, fish sauce, and lime juice.

■ Serves two.

Pla Jalamet Khao Neung Kiam Buai
(Steamed White Pompano with Pickled Plum)

INGREDIENTS :

1	white pompano weighing about 1 lb.
2	pickled plums
1/2	cup long, thin strips of pork fat
2	celery plants (see page 20)
1/2	cup rice-straw mushrooms
1	tsp. light soy sauce
1	tsp. shredded ginger
1	red chilli, sliced lengthwise into thin strips

PREPARATION:

■ Clean and wash the fish. With a knife, make several cuts on each side in a criss-cross design. Place the fish on a platter for steaming.

■ Mix the pork fat strips with the pickled plums and soy sauce and then pour over the fish.

■ Slice the mushrooms and the celery into short lengths. Place these and the chilli and ginger on the fish.

■ Place the platter containing the fish in a steamer in which the water is already boiling. Steam at high heat for about 15 minutes.

■ Serves two.

Si-Khrong Mu Phat Priao Wan

(Sweet and Sour Spareribs)

INGREDIENTS :

2	lbs. spareribs, cut into 1 1/2 inch lengths and marinated 2-3 hours in 1 tbsp. light soy sauce, 1 tsp. ground pepper, 1 tsp. salt, 1 tsp. corn flour, and 1 tsp. Chinese wine
1/4	cup chilli, sliced diagonally
1/2	cup pineapple, sliced into cubes
1/2	cup onion rings
1/4	cup tomato, cut in quarters

INGREDIENTS FOR THE SWEET AND SOUR SAUCE :

1/2	cup tomato catsup
1/4	cup shredded fresh young ginger
1	tbsp. vinegar
1	tbsp. sugar
1	tsp. salt
1/2	tsp. pepper
3	cups soup stock

PREPARATION:

■ Fry the marinated spareribs until golden brown in 1/2 cup cooking oil; then, remove from the pan and drain.

■ Mix the ingredients for the sweet and sour sauce in a pot, heat to boiling, then simmer about 15 minutes. Strain the sauce to remove any lumps. When ready to serve:

■ Place the fried pork ribs on a platter.

■ Heat 1/4 cup oil in a wok until very hot. Put the chillies, pineapple, tomatoes, and onions into the wok and fry. Add 1 cup of the sweet and sour sauce. In a bowl, mix 2 tbsp. corn starch with 3 tbsp. cold water, and add, as much of this as required to the mixture in the pan to thicken it; then, spoon it over the spareribs.

■ Serves four to five.

Phat Mu Priao Wan
(Sweet and Sour Pork)

INGREDIENTS :

1	lb. lean pork, sliced into thin 2″ × 1″ strips
3	oz. straw mushrooms, sliced
1	large tomato, sliced
1	cup 1-inch lengths of spring onion
1	tsp. chopped garlic
2	fresh chillies, deseeded and sliced
1/2	cup chicken stock
1	tbsp. vinegar
2	tbsp. tomato sauce
2	tbsp. sugar
1	tbsp. vegetable oil
1	tbsp. fish sauce
1	tbsp. tapioca flour
1/4	tbsp. pepper
1/3	cup sliced onion
1/4	tsp. salt
1	tbsp. chopped coriander greens
1/2	cup sliced cucumber

PREPARATION:

■ Heat the oil in a wok over medium-high heat and brown the garlic. Add the pork and cook for 5 minutes, stirring constantly. Then, add the mushrooms, tomato, spring onions, chillies, vinegar, tomato sauce, sugar, fish sauce, onions, salt and half of the chicken stock. Stir well.

■ Mix the remaining chicken stock with the tapioca flour, blend well and pour slowly into the wok and cook until the sauce thickens. Season with pepper and remove from heat. Garnish with coriander and cucumber.

■ Serves four.

Kung Op Wun Sen
(Baked Prawns and Mungbean Noodles)

INGREDIENTS :

1	lb. prawns
5	coriander roots, crushed
1	tbsp. pepper corns
1	onion, thinly sliced
3	slices ginger, crushed
2	tbsp. cooking oil
1	tbsp. Maggi sauce
1/4	tsp. salt
1	tbsp. sugar
1	tbsp. oyster sauce
2	tbsp. light soy sauce
1	tsp. sesame oil
1	tbsp. whiskey
2	cups mungbean noodles, soaked and cut into short lengths

PREPARATION:

■ Place the oil in a wok, heat, and stir fry the coriander root, ginger, pepper, and onion. When fragrant, remove from the wok and place in a mixing bowl.

■ Add the noodles, the sauces, salt, sugar, seasame oil and whiskey, toss the noodles until well coated, and then add the prawns and toss well once again.

■ Divide the noodles and prawns into four individual portions; place each portion in a lidded cup, and close the lids. Place the cups on a baking tray and bake at 450° F. until the prawns are done (about 10 minutes).

■ Serve hot with fresh vegetables, such as tomatoes and spring onions.

■ Serves four.

Kung Neung Si lu

(Prawns Steamed with Soy Sauce)

INGREDIENTS :

12	prawns
2	tsp. light soy sauce
2	coriander roots, chopped
1	tsp. oyster sauce
1	tbsp. chopped garlic
1	tbsp. finely chopped spring onion
1/4	tsp. pepper

PREPARATION:

■ Shell and devein the prawns and arrange on a plate.

■ Mix the garlic and coriander root with the soy sauce and the oyster sauce; then, pour over the prawns.

■ After the water has already begun to boil, place the prawns in the steamer. Steam about 10 minutes, remove, sprinkle with the spring onion and pepper, and serve.

■ Serves four.

Pla Samli Daet Diao
(Fried Sun-Dried Kingfish)

INGREDIENTS :

1	kingfish weighing 1 lb.-1 1/2 lbs.
1	tbsp. finely sliced shallot
2	tbsp. shredded green mango
1	tsp. shredded hot chilli
2	tbsp. fish sauce
3	tbsp. lime juice
1	tsp. palm sugar
2	cups cooking oil

PREPARATION:

■ Wash, clean and butterfly the fish leaving the two sides joined along the belly. Open the fish out flat so that the skin is downward, remove the bones, and score the flesh with a knife.

■ After allowing it to dry, lay the fish opened out flat in strong sunshine for five to six houres, turning regularly so the sun strikes both the skin side and the interior.

■ Pour the oil into a deep frying pan and place on a medium heat. When the oil is hot, place the fish, still opened out, in the oil. When the lower side becomes crisp and golden, turn the fish and continue frying until it is done on both sides; then, remove from the pan, drain, place on a serving dish.

■ Toss the shallots, mango, and chilli together, seasoning with fish sauce, lime juice, and palm sugar so that a sour taste is the predominant one. Spoon into a bowl and serve with the fish.

■ Serves two to three.

Pla Pae-Sa
(Steamed Fish)

INGREDIENTS :

1	fish weighing about 1 lb. (suitable are such meaty fish as serpent head)
1/4	cup shredded ginger
1/4	cup thin slices of pork fat
2	pickled garlic bulbs sliced thin
1	celery plant chopped into short lengths (see page 20)
1	red chilli sliced diagonally
2	cups chicken stock
3	tbsp. vinegar
2	tsp. sugar

PREPARATION:

■ Clean and scale the fish. Score it on both sides. Place it in a deep dish, lay the strips of pork fat upon it, and steam in a steamer on high heat for 10 minutes.

■ Remove the fish from the steamer and arrange upon it first, the celery, the pickled garlic, and then the chilli.

■ Mix the chicken stock, vinegar and sugar, stir until the sugar has dissolved, and then pour into the dish containing the fish. Return the dish to the steamer and steam over vigorously boiling water for about ten minutes; then, remove from the steamer and serve with the sauce.

INGREDIENTS FOR SAUCE :

5	hot chillies
1	tbsp. chopped crushed garlic
1	tbsp. sugar
2	tbsp. lime juice
1	tsp. finely ground roasted peanuts
1	tsp. salt

PREPARATION:

■ Pound the chillies, garlic, sugar, and salt together in a mortar, mix in the peanuts and lime juice, transfer to a small bowl.

■ Serves two.

Kai Phat Kap Haeo
(Stir Fried Chicken with Water Chestnuts)

INGREDIENTS :

1	lb. chicken
1/4	cup cooking oil
1	garlic plant
4	slices fresh ginger
1/4	cup light soy sauce
1	tbsp. sherry
1	cup water
10	canned water chestnuts
1/2	tbsp. sugar
1	tbsp. coarsely chopped celery

PREPARATION:

■ Wash the garlic plant and cut into two-inch sections. Wash the chicken and cut into bite-sized chunks.

■ Heat the oil in a wok. When hot, put in the ginger and garlic plant together with the chicken, stir-fry until chicken is golden brown. Add the soy sauce, the sherry and the water; then, cover the wok and reduce to low heat.

■ Add the water chestnuts and then the sugar; cook over low heat for 15 minutes until the chicken is tender. Then, spoon onto a serving platter, sprinkle with the celery, and serve hot.

■ Serves four.

Phat Khi Mao Kai reu Mu
(Spicy Stir-Fried Chicken or Pork)

INGREDIENTS :

5	hot chillies
4	coriander roots
2	tbsp. fish sauce
1	tbsp. oyster sauce
2	tbsp. cooking oil
5	cloves garlic
1/2	cup whole basil leaves (ka-prao)
1	tsp. sugar
2	cups ground chicken or pork

chicken stock

PREPARATION:

■ Pound the garlic, chilies, and coriander roots well in a mortar.

■ Heat the oil in a wok. When the oil is hot, add the pounded chilli mixture and stir-fry. When the garlic is golden brown, add the meat and continue stirring and turning.

■ When the meat is done, add the oyster sauce, fish sauce, sugar, and enough chicken stock to give the dish some liquid. Add the basil leaves and stir. Serve with rice.

■ Serves four.

Phat Phet Mu
(Stir-Fried Pork with Red Curry Paste)

INGREDIENTS :

1	lb. lean pork sliced into thin strips about 1 inch wide and 2 inches long
1	tbsp. red curry paste (See p. 26)
3	kaffir lime leaves torn in half
1	tbsp. green pepper corns
1	cup coconut milk
1/2	cup sweet basil leaves (horapha)
3/4	cup sliced baby zucchini
1 1/2	tbsp. fish sauce
1/4	tsp. salt
1	tbsp. sugar
1	tbsp. vegetable oil
2	fresh red chillies, deseeded and sliced

PREPARATION:

■ Heat oil in wok over medium heat. Fry the red curry paste and pork for 5 minutes, stirring regularly. Add half of the coconut milk and cook for another 10 minutes, stirring occasionally.

■ When the pork is done, add the remaining coconut milk, the fish sauce, kaffir lime leaves, salt and sugar, stir well and bring to a boil.

■ Then, add the zucchini, pepper corns and chillies, and stir well.

■ Garnish with basil.

■ Serves four.

Phat Phrik Khing Mu Kap Thua Fak Yao
(Savory Stir-Fried Pork with Yard-long Beans)

INGREDIENTS FOR CURRY PASTE :

3	dried chillies
7	shallots
2	garlic bulbs
1	tsp. galangal
1	tbsp. chopped lemon grass
5	pepper corns
1	tsp. chopped coriander root
1	tsp. grated kaffir lime rind
1	tsp. salt
1	tsp. shrimp paste
2	tbsp. ground dried shirmp

OTHER INGREDIENTS :

1	lb. pork
1/2	lb. yard-long beans
2	tbsp. cooking oil
1	tbsp. palm sugar
2	tbsp. fish sauce

PREPARATION:

- Place the chilli paste ingredients in a mortar and pound until thoroughly ground and mixed.
- Wash the pork, cut into long, thin slices, and marinate in 1 tbsp. fish sauce.
- Wash the beans, cut into 1 inch lengths, boil until just cooked, and remove from the water.
- Heat the oil in a wok, fry the pork until done, then remove the pork from the pan and set aside.
- Put the chilli paste in the wok and fry until fragrant, then add the pork, sugar, fish sauce, and yard-long beans. Stir-fry until thoroughly mixed, remove from heat and serve.
- Serves four.

Phat Phrik Khing Kai

(Savory Stir-Fried Chicken)

INGREDIENTS :

phrik khing curry paste (see the facing page)

1/2	cup coconut milk
1 1/2	lbs. sliced chicken breast
1/4	lb. bacon, fried crisp
4	kaffir lime leaves, torn into quarters
3	tbsp. vegetable oil
2	tbsp. fish sauce
1	tbsp.sugar

PREPARATION:

■ Put oil into a wok over medium heat. Add the phrik khing curry paste and stir well. Next add the coconut milk and chicken, stirring regularly until the chicken is done. Then add the kaffir lime leaves, fish sauce and sugar to taste. Remove from the heat and sprinkle with bacon.

■ Serves four.

Kha Mu Tom Phalo
(Boiled Fresh Ham with the Five Spices)

INGREDIENTS :

1 1/2	lbs. fresh ham
10	cloves garlic
3	coriander roots
1/2	tsp. five spice powder
20	pepper corns
1	tsp. dark soy sauce
2	tbsp. chilli sauce
2	tbsp. light soy sauce

PREPARATION:

■ Place all the ingredients in a pressure cooker and add enough water to nearly cover the ham (about 2 cups). Cover and cook about 20 minutes over medium heat. After removing the pressure cooker from the heat, allow it to cool (at least 10 minutes) before opening. Remove the bone from the ham, place the meat and the liquid in a serving dish and sprinkle with chopped coriander greens. Serve with the sauce.

INGREDIENTS FOR SAUCE :

2	yellow chillies
1	coriander root
10	cloves garlic
1/2	tsp. salt
2	tbsp. vinegar

PREPARATION:

■ Place the chillies, coriander root, garlic, and salt in a mortar and break up with the pestle. Mix in the vinegar and transfer to a small bowl.

■ Serves four to six.

Mu Tom Khem
(Stewed Pork)

INGREDIENTS :

2	lbs. tenderloin of pork (cut into cubes)
1	tsp. salt
1	tbsp. pepper corns
1	tbsp. chopped garlic
1	tbsp. chopped fresh coriander root
1	tbsp. brandy
3	tbsp. fish sauce
1	tbsp. vegetable oil
1/4	cup dark soy sauce
1 1/2	tbsp. palm sugar
2	cups water (or chicken broth)
4	shelled hard-boiled eggs

PREPARATION:

■ Into a blender put the pepper corns, coriander root, garlic, dark soy sauce, fish sauce, salt, palm sugar, brandy, and 1 cup of water, and blend well. Marinate the pork in this mixture for 20 minutes.

■ Heat oil in a wok over high heat and stir fry the pork with the marinade. Then, add 1 cup of water and the eggs, lower the heat, and simmer for 20 minutes.

■ Serves four to six.

Phat Neua Namman Hoi
(Stir-Fried Beef in Oyster Sauce)

INGREDIENTS :

1	lb. thin slices of tender beef
1	tbsp. wheat flour
3	tbsp. cooking oil
1	tsp. sugar
1/2	tsp. pepper
5	oz. straw mushrooms or champignons
2	tbsp. light soy sauce
4	tbsp. oyster sauce
1	spring onion cut into short lengths
1	tbsp. finely chopped garlic

PREPARATIONS:

■ Marinate the beef slices in a mixture of the flour and light soy sauce.

■ Place the oil in a wok over medium heat. Fry the garlic until fragrant and then add the mushrooms. When the mushrooms are tender, put in the beef and continue stir-frying until it is done.

■ Add the oyster sauce, sugar, and pepper, stir to mix well, add the spring onion, stir well and serve.

■ Serves three to four.

Phat Kha-na Namman Hoi
(Stir-Fried Kai Lan in Oyster Sauce)

INGREDIENTS :

10	kai lan plants of equal size
20	champignons or rice-straw mushrooms
3	tbsp. cooking oil
1	tbsp. finely chopped garlic
4	tbsp. oyster sauce
1	tsp. salt
1/4	tsp. pepper
1	tsp. sugar

PREPARATION:

■ Wash the kai lan well, remove the old leaves, the old part of the stem, and the tough outer covering of the stem.

■ Wash the mushrooms and remove any inedible portions.

■ To boiling water, add 1 tsp. salt. Parboil kai lan, remove from hot water immediately and submerge in cold water. Scald the mushrooms in a similar manner. Drain both the kai lan and the mushrooms.

■ Heat the oil in a wok. When it is hot, fry the garlic. When it is fragrant, add the kai lan and the mushrooms, stir to mix well, and then add the chicken stock, oyster sauce, sugar, and pepper. Stir well, remove from heat and serve.

■ Serves four.

Phat Ma-kheua Yao
(Stir-Fried Chicken with Long Eggplant)

INGREDIENTS :

1/2	lb. chicken breast, deboned and sliced
1	cup sliced long eggplant
1/3	cup sweet basil leaves (horapha)
2	fresh chillies, deseeded and sliced
1/2	tbsp. chopped garlic
1/2	tbsp. soybean paste
1	tbsp. fish sauce
1	tbsp. dark soy sauce
2	vegetable oil
3	tbsp. water (or chicken stock)

PREPARATION:

■ Heat oil in a wok over medium heat. Fry the garlic. When it yellows put in the chicken and cook for 5 minutes. Then, add eggplant and cook for another 5 minutes. Stir in the soybean paste, fish sauce, and dark soy sauce, and cook for 2 minutes. Add the water (or chicken stock), chillies, and basil and slowly bring to a boil. Remove from heat and serve.

■ Serves four.

Phat Phak Anamai
(Stir-Fried Prawns with Vegetables)

INGREDIENTS :

1	young sponge gourd
10	ears baby corn
10	rice-straw mushrooms or champignons
12	prawns
1	tbsp. chopped garlic
3	tbsp. cooking oil
1/2	tsp. salt
3	tbsp. oyster sauce

PREPARATION:

■ Peel and wash the sponge gourd and cut into bite-sized pieces. Slice the baby corn and rice-straw mushrooms in half. If champignons are used, scald them before slicing. Shell and devein the prawns.

■ Heat the oil in a wok. When it is hot, put in the garlic. When the garlic is fragrant, add the prawns and salt. When the prawns are done, add the baby corn and then the mushrooms. When the mushrooms are done, add the sponge gourd and fry until cooked. Add the oyster sauce and stir thoroughly. Serve hot.

■ Serves four.

Phat Himalai
(Stir-Fried Chicken with Cashew Nut)

INGREDIENTS :

1	lb. sliced chicken breast
1/2	cup freshly roasted cashew nuts
1/4	cup fried dried chillies
1/3	cup chopped spring onion
1/2	tbsp. chopped garlic
1 1/2	tbsp. fish sauce
1	tbsp. dark soy sauce
1/4	tsp. salt
2	tbsp. vegetable oil
1	small onion, sliced

PREPARATION:

■ Heat oil in wok over medium heat. Fry the garlic. When it has yellowed, add the chicken and cook for 5 minutes, turning regularly. Then, add the roasted cashew nuts, chilies, onion, spring onions, fish sauce, dark soy sauce, and salt and cook 1 minute. Garnish with the chopped spring onions.

■ Serves four.

Phat Thua Ngok Kap Mu Krop

(Stir-Fried Bean Sprouts and Crisp-Fried Roasted Pork Belly)

INGREDIENTS :

1	lb. bean sprouts
1/2	lb. crisp-fried roasted pork belly
2	tbsp. light soy sauce
3	tbsp. cooking oil
1	tsp. chopped garlic

PREPARATION:

■ Wash the bean sprouts well and then drain in a colander.

■ Slice the pork into bite-sized pieces.

■ Heat the oil in a wok. When the oil is hot, fry the garlic until golden brown; then, add the pork and the bean sprouts, mix, add the soy sauce, stir, and remove from the heat. Avoid over cooking. Serve hot.

INGREDIENTS FOR CRISP-FRIED ROASTED PORK BELLY :

1	tsp. salt
1	tbsp. maggi sauce
2	cups cooking oil
1	lb. pork belly

PREPARATION:

■ Cut the pork belly into half-inch thick strips and marinate in a mixture of the salt and maggi sauce for two hours.

■ Place the strips one next to another in a roasting pan and roast in a 350°F. oven for 30 minutes.

■ Heat the oil in a deep wok. Deep fry the pork strips until the skin is golden brown; then, remove from the oil and drain.

■ Serves four.

Pet Thot Sot Sai
(Baked Stuffed Duck)

INGREDIENTS :

1	deboned duck with innards
2 1/2	cups chopped pork
1	egg
2	tbsp. pounded mixture of garlic, coriander root and pepper
1/4	cup diced onion
1/4	cup diced carrot
1/4	cup peas
3	tbsp. light soy sauce
2	tbsp. Maggi sauce
2	tbsp. butter
1	tbsp. sugar

INGREDIENTS FOR GRAVY :

1/4	cup juices from the pan in which the duck was baked
1	tbsp. wheat flour
1/4	tsp. salt
1/8	tsp. pepper

PREPARATION:

■ Wash the duck and remove the innards. Dice the liver, gizzard, heart, and whatever other organs you like. Using a sharp knife with a small, pointed blade debone the duck. Try to keep as much meat as possible and avoid puncturing the meat with the knife. Start near the vent and work up one side toward the neck. Remove the neck and continue around the neck across the back of the duck. Then, follow the same procedure on the other side. Lift the skeleton free of the flesh and then remove the bones from the legs. When done, turn the duck right side out (see p. 22).

■ Mix the pork, pounded garlic mixture, diced innards, peas, carrots, and onion together well, add the egg and mix, season with light soy sauce and maggi sauce. Fill the cavities of the duck with the mixture, sew the duck closed, and tie securely with the thread around the outside into a long, cigar-shaped configuration.

■ Place the duck in a baking pan and bake at 350°F. for 40 minutes. Remove the duck from the oven, spread the butter over the outside, and bake at 400° F. for 20 minutes. When the back of the duck has turned dark brown, remove from the oven, allow to cool, and cut into 1/2-inch slices.

■ Place the slices on a bed of lettuce on a serving platter, surround with slices of pineapple, tomato, and cucumber, and spoon gravy over the duck.

PREPARATION:

■ Heat the duck juices in a wok over low heat. Add the flour, salt, and pepper and stir until the gravy is smooth.

■ Serves six to eight.

Ped Yang
(Crispy Duck)

INGREDIENTS :

1	duck weighing about 4 lbs.
2	tsp. minced mature ginger
1	tsp. ground cinnamon
1/2	tsp. nutmeg
1	tsp. pepper
2	tbsp. light soy sauce

PREPARATION:

■ Wash the duck, remove the neck, feet, and innards, and pat dry.

■ Mix the ginger, cinnamon, nutmeg, and pepper. Take 1 tsp. of this mixture and spread it over the inside of the duck; then, sew the duck securely closed. Spread the remainder of the spice mixture over the outside of the duck.

■ Wrap the duck in aluminum foil, place it in a deep roasting pan, bake at 450° F. for one hour. After taking the duck from the overn, allow it to cool about fifteen minutes before removing the aluminum foil.

■ Place the duck on a roasting rack and put it on a cookie sheet. With a fork, puncture the skin of the duck at many places over the entire surface in order to prevent the skin's cracking.

■ Bake the duck at 375°F. for about 30 minutes. Remove the duck from the oven and brush the skin with the light soy sauce. Now, bake at 500°F. for about 5 minutes, until the skin is crisp and brown. Do not allow it to burn.

■ Serve the duck either split in half or deboned. Alternatively, the skin may be served without the meat. Serve with spring onions, cucumbers, lettuce, celery and dark soy sauce.

■ Serves six.

Mu Yang
(Barbecued Pork)

INGREDIENTS :

2	lb. pork shoulder cut into 2 × 4 × 4 inch pieces
2	tbsp. light soy sauce
2	tbsp. sherry
1	tbsp. sesame oil
4	tbsp. sugar
1	tsp. salt
2	garlic plants cut into 1 inch lengths
2	tsp. juice from freshly pounded ginger
2	tbsp. honey

PREPARATION:

■ Marinate pork in the other ingredients about six hours before barbecuing.

■ While barbecuing, brush pork with marinade. When done, cut pork into small pieces and arrange on a platter. Serve with **sweet chilli sauce** (see following recipe) and fresh vegetables such as spring onion, slices of cucumber and tomato.

■ Serves four to five.

Kai Yang
(Thai-Style Barbecued Chicken)

INGREDIENTS :

2	lbs. chicken pieces
2	tbsp. chopped fresh ginger
2	tbsp. chopped lemon grass
2	tbsp. chopped coriander root
2	cups light soy sauce
1	tsp. sugar
2	tbsp. pepper
1 1/2	tbsp. curry powder

PREPARATION:

■ Mix all the ingredients, except the chicken, in a blender and marinate the chicken in the mixture for at least 6 hours in a refrigerator.

■ Broil the chicken slowly over a low fire and serve with sweet chilli sauce.

INGREDIENTS FOR SWEET CHILLI SAUCE :

1	tbsp. ground red chilli
1/2	cup vinegar
1	tsp. salt
1	tbsp. sugar
1	tsp. chopped garlic

PREPARATION:

■ Mix all the ingredients in a small pot, put over a medium heat and bring to a boil, stirring. Heat until thickened to a syrupy consistency then remove from heat.

■ Serves four to five.

Neua Daet Diao
(Fried Sun-Dried Beef)

INGREDIENTS :

1	lb. beef	1	tbsp. fish sauce
1	garlic bulb	3	coriander roots
1	tsp. curry powder	1	tbsp. sugar
1/2	tsp. pepper	2	tbsp. whiskey
1	tbsp. oyster sauce	3	tbsp. chilli sauce

PREPARATION:

■ After washing the beef, cut it into slices about 1/3 inch thick.

■ Pound the garlic, coriander root, and pepper in a mortar. Add the beef slices and work them around in the mixture. Add the fish sauce, oyster sauce, whiskey, sugar, and curry powder, mix well, and allow to marinate for one hour.

■ Arrange the slices of beef on a rack and leave in the sun for one day. Turn occasionally.

■ Fry the sun-dried beef in hot oil and then drain. Serve with sweet chilli sauce (see previous recipe).

■ Serves four.

Si-Khrong Mu Yang
(Barbecued Spareribs)

INGREDIENTS :

2 1/2	lbs. spareribs	1/4	tsp. ground nutmeg
3	tbsp. light soy sauce	1/4	tsp. ground cinnamon
1	tsp. salt	1 1/2	tbsp. minced ginger
3	tbsp. whiskey	1	tsp. pepper

PREPARATION:

■ Cut the spareribs into pieces about 5 inches long and about 3 inches — or three ribs — wide.

■ Sprinkle the soy sauce and whiskey onto the spareribs so as to wet all surfaces. Mix the salt, nutmeg, cinnamon, ginger, and pepper together and then smear the mixture onto the ribs, covering them completely. Set aside to marinate for an hour.

■ Broil the spareribs over a slow charcoal fire until the meat is done and the outside is crisp.

■ Cut the ribs into 2 inch pieces and serve with cucumber, pineapple, spring onions and lettuce. Serve with sweet chilli sauce (see previous recipe).

■ Serves four.

Phat-Thai
(Thai Fried Noodles)

INGREDIENTS :

7	oz. narrow rice noodles, soaked and drained
3	tbsp. cooking oil
1	tbsp. chopped garlic
1	egg
4	tbsp. diced firm yellow beancurd
3	oz. prawns, shelled and deveined
1/2	tbsp. pickled Chinese radish
3	tbsp. sugar
2	tbsp. fish sauce
4	tbsp. vinegar
1/2	tbsp. paprika
2	tbsp. chopped roasted peanuts
6	oz. bean sprouts
1/3	cup spring onions, cut into 1" lengths
1/4	tsp. ground chilli
1	fresh lime, sliced

PREPARATION:

■ In a large frying pan, heat oil over medium-high heat, sauté the garlic and pickled radish for 1 minute; then, add the egg and keep stirring. Add the prawns, beancurd and the noodles; then, season with sugar, fish sauce, vinegar, paprika and 1 tbsp. peanuts. Toss and cook for 10 minutes, until noodles turn soft. Then, add the spring onions, ground chilli and half of the bean sprouts, and remove from heat. Garnish with 1 tbsp. of chopped roasted peanuts.

■ Serve with the remaining bean sprouts with the lime on the side.

■ Serves two.

Sen Jan Phat Kung

(Stir-Fried Rice Noodles and Prawns)

INGREDIENTS :

1/2	lb. prawns shelled and deveined
1/2	cup sliced shallots
2	tbsp. sliced garlic
5	dried chillies, seeds removed, soaked in water
1/4	cup palm sugar
1/4	cup tamarind juice
1/4	cup fish sauce
1	oz. bean sprouts
4	oz. Chinese chives (see page 20)
1/4	cup cooking oil
2-3	limes
10	oz. dried narrow rice noodles (Chanthaburi noodles), soaked about 5 minutes in water

PREPARATION:

■ Slice the dried chillies. Place the chillies and the salt in a mortar and pound, then add the garlic and shallots and pound until ground and mixed throughly.

■ Heat the oil in a wok. When hot, fry the pounded chilli paste. Add the prawns and fry, turning regularly until done.

■ Add the noodles, turning for a few minutes. Then, add the bean sprouts, and Chinese chives cut into short lengths, and mix.

■ Serve with banana flower, Chinese chives, bean sprouts and wedges of lime.

■ Serves two to three.

Khao Phat Mu Kung Sai Khai
(Fried Rice with Pork, Shrimp and Egg)

INGREDIENTS :

1 1/2	cups rice
5	oz. pork
5	oz. shrimp, shelled and deveined
2	eggs
1/4	cup cooking oil
1	onion
2	tbsp. catsup
1	tbsp. sugar
3	tbsp. light soy sauce
1	coriander plant
1	red chilli
2	cucumbers
6	spring onions
2	limes

PREPARATION:

■ Steam the rice using 2 1/2 cups water for about 40 minutes. When the rice is done, rake it to separate the grains.

■ Cut the pork into small pieces and marinate in 1 tbsp. light soy sauce for a few minutes.

■ Cut the onion into slices about 1/5 inch thick.

■ Heat the oil in a wok; when the oil is hot, fry the onions and then the pork, shrimp, catsup, sugar, and soy sauce. Sauté until the pork is done and then add the rice. Continue stirring the rice, scraping the bottom of the wok regularly to guard against sticking, until the desired degree of dryness is reached; then, remove the rice from the wok.

■ Return the wok to the heat, add 1 tbsp. of oil, allow it to heat and then break the eggs into the wok. With the spatula, break, spread, and turn the eggs, and when done, cut into strips, remove from the wok, and mix with the fried rice.

■ Peel the cucumbers and cut into discs. Slice the chilli into long shreds.

■ Put the fried rice on a plate, sprinkle with chopped coriander and shreds of chilli, and serve with cucmber, spring onions, and wedges of lime.

■ Serves four.

Khao Rat Na Kai

(Chicken in Sauce on Rice)

INGREDIENTS :

1	lb. rice
1	lb. chicken
4	oz. chicken livers
1	onion
3	oz. pineapple, cut into small pieces
3	oz. cherry tomatoes, halved
4	oz. Chinese mustard greens (phak kwangtung)
1	cup (4 oz.) spring onions cut into 1 inch lengths
2	coriander plants, roots removed
3	tbsp. light soy sauce
2 1/2	cup chicken stock
3	tbsp. tapioca flour mixed in 1/4 cup water
1	tsp. sugar
1	tbsp. chopped garlic
2	tbsp. cooking oil
1/2	tsp. pepper
3	chillies
1/4	cup vinegar
2	green bell peppers

PREPARATION:

■ Wash the rice, divide into five portions, and place each in a steaming cup. Add 2/3 cup water to each cup and steam until done.

■ Cut the chicken meat and livers into small slices and marinate in 1 tbsp. light soy sauce.

■ Peel and wash onion, cut in half, then cut into thin slices.

■ Heat oil in a wok, brown the garlic, then add the chicken meat and livers and fry until done. Add the onion slices. When cooked, add the mushrooms, mustard greens, and hot chicken stock. Add light soy sauce and sugar to taste and thicken with the tapioca flour in water. When boiling, taste and season as necessary, then add the spring onions and remove from heat.

■ Invert the cups of steamed rice on serving plates and tap to remove rice. Spoon the hot Chicken sauce over the rice, decorate with shredded green bell peppers, sprinkle with pepper, and serve immediately.

■ Serve with the chilli cut into thin rings soaked in vinegar.

■ Serves five.

Khao Man Kai
(Chicken with Rice Cooked in Chicken Broth)

INGREDIENTS :

2	chicken breasts or thighs (1 lb.)
3	cups water .
1	tsp. salt
2	crushed coriander roots
1 1/2	cups rice
3	tbsp. cooking oil
10	slightly crushed garlic cloves
5	cucumbers (see page 21)
1	coriander plant, root removed

PREPARATION:

■ Place the chicken in a pot with the 3 cups water, salt, and coriander roots and boil until the chicken is done. Skim off any froth, and use low heat to get a clear broth. Remove the chicken from the pot, debone it, and cut into thin slices. Strain the broth.

■ Wash the rice, pour off water, and allow to stand a while.

■ Heat the oil in a wok and add garlic. Before the garlic browns, add the rice and fry 3 minutes. Place the rice into a pot, add 2 1/2 cups chicken broth, and cook until the rice is done.

■ Spoon the rice onto plates, arrange the chicken slices on top and garnish with coriander. Slice the cucumbers into 1/4 inch discs and put on the sides of the plates. Serve with fermented soybean sauce.

INGREDIENTS FOR FERMENTED SOYBEAN SAUCE :

3	tbsp. fermented soybeans
1	tsp. dark soy sauce
1	tbsp. vinegar
1	tsp. sugar
1	tbsp. mature ginger, well pounded
1	chilli, well pounded

PREPARATION:

■ Strain the fermented soybeans and collect the liquid. Pound the solid portion thoroughly and mix with the liquid. Mix in the soy sauce, vinegar, sugar, ginger, and chilli. Spoon into small dishes.

■ Serves three.

Khao Phat Kapi
(Stir-Fried Rice and Shrimp Paste)

INGREDIENTS :

3	cups cooked rice
1	cup thinly sliced pork
1	tbsp. shrimp paste
1	tbsp. water
1	tbsp. fish sauce
4	shallots sliced thin
1	tbsp. minced garlic
3	tbsp. fried dried shrimp
2	limes
1	tsp. sugar
1	cup cooking oil
1	egg
1	coriander plant, coarsely chopped
1	red chilli sliced thin
6	cucumbers (see page 21)

INGREDIENTS FOR SWEET PORK :

1/2	cup pork, thinly sliced
2	tbsp. palm sugar
1	tbsp. chopped garlic
1	tbsp. fish sauce
2	tsp. dark soy sauce
2	tbsp. cooking oil
1/4	cup water

PREPARATION:

■ Fry the garlic in a wok. Add the pork, and when it is done, mix the water with the shrimp paste and add to the wok. Add the sugar and fish sauce and reduce the heat.

■ Add the rice and stir with the spatula to mix well. When the rice is hot, add the shallots, mix thoroughly, and remove from the wok.

■ Beat the egg. Place 1 tbsp. oil in a wok and heat. When the wok is hot, spread the oil, pour in the egg, and spread it in a thin layer over the wok. When set well, remove from the wok, roll up, and cut into thin slices.

■ Spoon portions of the rice onto plates, add egg, sweet pork and dried shrimp, sprinkle with coriander and chilli, and serve with cucumber slices and wedges of lime.

PREPARATION:

■ Mix the pork and the garlic. Fry the pork in the cooking oil until the pork is just done.

■ Add the fish sauce, dark soy sauce and sugar, stirring regularly. Add the water. Cover the wok and simmer until the water is dried. Remove from heat.

■ Serves three to four.

Khao Op Kun Chiang
(Chinese Sausage Steamed in Rice)

INGREDIENTS :

2	cups rice
2	Chinese sausages (kun chiang)
3 1/2	oz. lean pork
6	oz. small prawns
3	Shiitake mushrooms, soaked in water
2	tbsp. oyster sauce
2	tbsp. light soy sauce
10	cloves garlic, chopped
4	tbsp. cooking oil
1	tip of ginger root, diced

PREPARATION:

■ Slice the sausage. Cut the pork into small thin strips. Shell and clean the prawns.

■ After the mushrooms have absorbed water and filled out, cut them into thin slices. Save the water in which the mushrooms were soaked.

■ Wash and drain the rice.

■ Place the oil in a wok over medium heat. When it is hot, put in the garlic and ginger and fry, stirring long enough for the flavors to come out; then, add the sausage. When the sausage is hot and fragrant, add the pork, prawns, and mushrooms. Stir, adding the rice and then the oyster sauce and soy sauce. Work with the spatula until all the ingredients are thoroughly mixed; then, transfer the mixture to a pot.

■ Add enough water to the water in which the mushrooms were soaked to obtain a total of three cups, add this to the pot, and then place the pot on the heat.

■ Cooking time is about 30-35 minutes. Toward the end, cover the pot and reduce the heat. When the rice is done, remove from the heat and allow the rice to stand for a time in the covered pot. Spoon onto plates and serve with pineapple or fresh vegetables, such as cabbage and spring onions.

■ Serves four.

Neua Tun

(Stewed Beef)

INGREDIENTS :

1	lb. beef shank
10	cups water
1	cm. length of cinnamon, broken into small pieces
1/2	inch length of galangal
3	coriander roots
2	tbsp. light soy sauce
1	tbsp. dark soy sauce
1/2	tsp. salt
1	bay leaf (krawan leaf)
2	celery plants(see page 20)
7	oz. lettuce, swamp cabbage, or bean sprouts
2	tbsp. fried garlic
1/2	tsp. ground black pepper
1	tbsp. chopped fresh coriander

PREPARATION:

■ Wash the meat, cut into 1 inch cubes, place in pot.

■ Add the water, cinnamon, galangal, coriander roots, light soy sauce, dark soy sauce, salt, and bay leaf.

■ Heat to a boil, then cover, reduce heat, and simmer until the meat is tender. (If using an ordinary pot, this will be 3-4 hours. With a pressure cooker use only 2 cups of water and cook for 25 minutes, then remove from heat, allow to cool, open lid, and add 3 cups boiled water. Season to taste and bring to a boil once again).

■ Blanch the vegetables, cut into 1 inch pieces and place on the bottom of the serving bowl. Pour the stewed beef on top of the vegetables, sprinkle with coarsely cut fresh coriander, celery, fried garlic and ground pepper. Serve with steamed rice or noodles.

■ Serves four.

Khanom Jin Nam Ya
(Vermicelli and Fish Sauce)

INGREDIENTS FOR SPICE MIXTURE :

7	shallots, cut up coarsely
2	garlic gloves
2	tsp. sliced galangal
2	tbsp. sliced lemon grass
1	cup minced krachai
3	dried chillies, seeds removed
1	tsp. salt
1	tsp. shrimp paste
1	one-inch thick piece of salted fish, roasted
1	cup water

OTHER INGREDIENTS :

2	lbs. grated coconut or 5 cups coconut milk
1	meaty fish (1 lb.)
2-3	tbsp. fish sauce
2	hard boiled eggs, each peeled and cut into 5 sections
2	lbs. vermicelli
4	oz. yard-long beans, cut into short lengths and boiled a short time
4	oz. boiled swamp cabbage, cut into thin slices
4	oz. boiled bean sprouts
1	cup sweet basil leaves (maenglak)
1	chilli
ground dried chillies	

PREPARATION:

- Place all the spice mixture ingredients in a pot and simmer over low heat until tender. Remove from heat, cool, place in mortar or blender and pound or blend to a fine paste.

- Add 2 1/2 cups warm water to the grated coconut and squeeze out 5 cups coconut milk. Skim off 1/2 cup coconut cream and set aside to add at the end.

- Wash and clean the fish, removing head and entrails, and boil until done in 1 cup water. Save the water in which the fish was boiled.

- Remove the meat from the fish, add to the blended spice mixture and blend thoroughly. Pour the mixture into a pot, mix in the coconut milk, and heat to boiling. Add the fish broth and fish sauce and simmer, stirring regularly to prevent sticking. When the sauce has thickened add the coconut cream and remove from the heat.

- Arrange the vermicelli, vegetables, and eggs on plates. Just before serving, spoon the hot sauce over the noodles.

Khanom Jin Nam Phrik
(Vermicelli and Prawn Sauce)

INGREDIENTS FOR SPICE MIXTURE :

2	tbsp. roasted shallots
2	tbsp. roasted garlic
1	tsp. roasted galangal
1	tbsp. chopped coriander root
1	dried small chillie

OTHER INGREDIENTS :

1	lb. grated coconut or 3 3/4 cups coconut milk
1	lb. prawns, shelled and deveined
2	oz. ground roasted shelled mungbeans
2	tbsp. chopped garlic
7	tbsp. ground dried chillie s
1/4	cup cooking oil
6	tbsp. fish sauce
6	tbsp. palm sugar
6	tbsp. lemon juice
1	lb. vermicelli
2	cups chopped green apple or raw papaya
2	cups sliced swamp cabbage or cabbage

PREPARATION:

- Pound the roasted garlic, shallots, galangal, coriander root and dried chillies in a mortar until well ground and thoroughly mixed.
- Add 2 1/2 cups warm water to the grated coconut and squeeze out 3 3/4 cups coconut milk. Skim off 1 cup coconut cream. Place coconut cream in a pot and heat until some oil surfaces, remove from heat and set aside.
- Heat 1 cup of the remaining coconut milk and 1 cup of water to boiling, add the prawns. When the prawns are done, remove them from the pot, place them in a mortar, and pound well.
- Add the remaining 1 3/4 cups of coconut milk to the pot in which the prawns were cooked. Add, a little at a time and stirring after each addition, the ground spice mixture along with the pounded prawns. Then, mix in the mungbeans and add the fish sauce, palm sugar, and lime juice to give the sauce a sour, sweet, and salty taste. Remove the pot from the heat.
- Sauté the chopped garlic in the cooking oil. When it begins to brown, remove the garlic from the oil, put in ground chilli and reduce the heat.
- When the oil has taken on a red color, transfer it to the pot containing the sauce, add the coconut milk set aside earlier, and sprinkle with the sautéed garlic.
- To serve, place four coils of vermicelli on each plate, add about 2 tbsp. of shredded papaya or apple and about 2 tbsp. of vegetable, and then spoon on about 1/2 cup of the sauce.

Ta-Ko
(Thai-Style Tapioca)

INGREDIENTS :

2 1/2	cups small tapioca pearls
3 1/4	cups water
1	cup sugar

TOPPING :

2	cups coconut milk
2	tsp. sugar
1/4	cup rice flour
1	tsp. salt

PREPARATION:

■ Wash and drain the tapioca pearls; transfer to a pot, add the sugar and water; boil about 20 minutes until done.

■ Spoon the tapioca into individual small bowls and top with a few spoonfuls of the coconut milk mixture.

TOPPING:

■ Mix together the coconut milk, salt, sugar and rice flour in another pot, place over medium-low heat and cook until the mixture thickens.

■ Serves four.

Khanom Mo Kaeng Pheuak
(Taro Coconut Custard)

INGREDIENTS :

1 1/2	cups mashed boiled taro
1 1/4	cups coconut milk
5	eggs, slightly beaten
1	tbsp. all-purpose flour
1/2	tsp. salt
1 1/4	cups palm sugar
1	tbsp. fried, thinly sliced shallot

PREPARATION:

■ In a mixing bowl, mix the coconut milk, flour and sugar well. Set aside.

■ In a separate bowl, mix the taro, eggs, and salt; beat until smooth.

■ Combine both mixtures in a pot and cook over medium heat for 5 minutes, then remove from heat.

■ Put this mixture in separate serving bowls, and bake in oven at 350 °F. for 35 minutes, or until golden brown on top. Garnish with the fried shallots.

■ Serves four.

Thua Khiao Tom Nam Tan
(Mungbeans in Syrup)

INGREDIENTS :

1	cup mungbeans
1	cup light brown sugar
5	cups water

PREPARATION:

■ Soak the mungbeans overnight or at least three hours, and then drain.

■ Boil the mungbeans in the 5 cups water until tender and then add the sugar. When the sugar has dissolved completely and the syrup has returned to a strong boil, remove from the heat.

■ Serves four.

Fak Thong Kaeng Buat
(Pumpkin in Coconut Cream)

INGREDIENTS :

2	lbs. pumpkin
4	cups coconut milk
1	cup sugar
1/2	tsp. salt
1	cup water

PREPARATION:

■ Wash the skin of the pumpkin clean. Remove some, but not all, of the skin; the outer surface need not be completely smooth. Remove the seeds and membrane from the inside and cut the flesh into uniform pieces about one-half inch thick.

■ Take 1 cup of the coconut milk, mix it with the sugar, salt, and the 1 cup water, heat to boiling, add the pumpkin, and continue cooking. When the pumpkin is tender, add the remaining coconut milk, bring to a boil once again, and remove from the heat. Serve in small bowls.

■ Serves four.

Khao Phot Piak
(Corn Pudding with Coconut Cream)

INGREDIENTS :

3	cups sliced kernels of corn	4	tbsp. tapioca flour or corn flour
2	cups water	1	cup coconut milk
1	cup sugar	1/2	tsp. salt.

PREPARATION:

- Heat the water to boiling, add the corn, and boil, stirring constantly, until tender (five to ten minutes).
- Add the sugar and the flour, stirring all the while, continue cooking. When smooth, remove from the heat.
- Add salt to the coconut milk, bring to a boil, and then remove from the heat.
- Place a portion of the corn pudding into individual dessert dishes and top with the coconut milk.
- Serves four.

Kluai Buat Chi
(Bananas in Coconut Cream)

INGREDIENTS :

10	ripe Nam Wa variety bananas (see page 17)
1/2	cup coconut cream
3	cups coconut milk
1	cup sugar
1	tsp. salt

PREPARATION:

- Peel the bananas and cut into quarters.
- Place the coconut milk in a pot and heat to boiling. Add the bananas and cook over a medium heat until tender; then, add the sugar and salt; stir until dissolved.
- Add the coconut cream, spoon into bowls, and serve.

   Khai-variety bananas may also be used.

   If the bananas are very ripe, reduce the amount of sugar used. If the bananas are not yet fully ripe, they may not be sweet and may have a certain astringency. If so, first boil the bananas in plain water. Remove them from the water, and then proceed as in the above recipe except that the sugar should be dissolved in the coconut milk before the bananas are added. This will reduce the astringency and give the bananas and coconut cream a more appetizing appearance.

- Serves four to five.

Man Tom Nam Tan
(Sweet Potatoes in Syrup)

INGREDIENTS :

1	lb. sweet potatoes
1	cup sugar
4-5	slices mature ginger

PREPARATION:

■ Peel the sweet potatoes, wash well, and slice them across into discs about one inch thick. Cut each disc into 4-6 wedges and soak in water.

■ Bring 4 cups water to a boil, add the sweet potato. When the pot comes to a boil once again, add the ginger and cook until the potato is tender. Then, add the sugar and leave on the heat until all the sugar has dissolved and the pot has returned to a good boil.

■ Serves four.

Man Cheuam
(Candied Sweet Potato)

INGREDIENTS :

1	lb. large sweet potatoes
1 1/2	cups sugar
2	cups water
1 1/2	cups limewater

PREPARATION:

■ Wash the sweet potatoes well and peel them. Cut them into pieces about 3/4-inch thick. (If the sweet potatoes are small, slice them lengthwise; if large, slice across into discs.) Soak the sweet potato in limewater about half an hour and then wash in clean water before candying.

■ Place 2 cups water in a sauce pan or a wok and heat. When the water is hot, add the sugar and stir until it dissolves. If necessary, filter the solution to remove foreign matter.

■ Now bring the sugar solution to a boil in a wok. Allow to boil about five minutes and then add the sweet potatoes. The sweet potatoes need not be stirred often; they should, however, be turned from time to time. Reduce the heat as the syrup thickens and contiue cooking until the syrup penetrates the potato completely.

■ Serves four.

Kluai Khaek
(Fried Bananas)

INGREDIENTS :

3/4	cup rice flour	1/2	cup grated coconut
1/4	cup tapioca flour	1-1 1/4	cups water
2	tbsp. sugar	10	Nam Wa variety bananas
1	tsp. salt	3	cups cooking oil

The bananas should be just ripening : still green but beginning to turn yellow. Fried sweet potato and fried taro may also be made following this recipe.

PREPARATION:

■ Mix the rice and tapioca flours, sugar, salt, and grated coconut; then, adding water a little at a time, knead the ingredients until thoroughly mixed and of the consistency of a fairly thick batter.

■ Peel the bananas and cut each one lengthwise into three or four slices.

■ Place the slices in the batter so that they are completely coated with it.

■ Place the oil in a deep wok over high heat. When the oil is hot, fry the bananas to a golden brown; then, remove from the oil and drain.

Khao Tom Mat
(Banana and Glutinous Rice Steamed in Banana Leaf)

INGREDIENTS :

banana leaf
1	cup black beans, boiled until soft
1	lb. glutinous rice (soaked for 30 minutes)
14	oz. grated coconut or 2 cups coconut milk
1/2	cup sugar
2	tbsp. salt
10	bananas (Nam Wa variety) (see page 17)

PREPARATION:

■ Wash and drain the rice.

■ Mix 1 cup warm water with the coconut and squeeze out 2 cups coconut milk.

■ Dissolve the sugar and salt in the coconut milk and strain into a pan, add the rice, then cook over low heat with constant stirring until mixture is dry.

■ Peel the bananas and slice in half lengthwixse.

■ Tear the banana leaf from edge to midrib into pieces 7-8 inches wide and place together in pairs so the midrib side of one is opposite that of the other. Put some rice on the leaf, place a half banana on the rice, cover the banana with more rice, press several black beans into the rice, then wrap up in the leaf. If desired, tie the packet; then, steam for 40-45 minutes.

If the rice has not been soaked, the packets must be tied securely and boiled for 1 hour.

Aisa-khrim Ka-thi
(Coconut Milk Ice Cream)

INGREDIENTS :

3 1/2   cups coconut milk
1   cup sugar
1/2   cup water

PREPARATION:

■ Place the sugar and water in a pot and heat until the sugar dissolves. If necessary, filter the solution through cheesecloth to remove any foreign matter and then return to the heat. Continue heating to obtain a syrup thick enough to stick to a wooden paddle; then, remove from the heat.

■ When the syrup has cooled somewhat but is still warm, add the coconut milk and stir to mix well.

■ Pour the solution into an ice cream freezer and crank about 45 minutes, or until stiff. Coconut milk ice cream must be kept cold because it melts rapidly.

■ To serve, scoop the ice cream into a dessert dish. You may sprinkle with 1 tbsp. roasted peanuts.

For variety, try adding shreds of ripe jackfruit or young coconut meat before putting the mixture into the ice cream freezer.

■ Note: freshly squeezed coconut milk will make the best ice cream. (See page 17)

■ Serves six.

Kafae Yen or Cha Yen
(Thai-Style Iced Coffee or Tea)

INGREDIENTS :

2	tbsp. ground coffee or powdered Thai tea leaves
1 1/2	cups boiling water
4	tbsp. sugar
1/4	cup unsweetened condensed milk

crushed ice or ice cubes

PREPARATION:

■ Place ground coffee or powered tea leaves in a cloth bag.

■ Place bag in a mug and pour the boiling water into the bag. Allow to steep a few moments, lift bag to a second mug, pour contents of the first mug into the bag, and repeat until desired strength is reacher.

■ Remove bag, add sugar and milk, stir until dissolved, and pour into ice-filled glasses.

■ Serves two.

INDEX

A

APPETIZERS

Coconut Milk and Fermented Soybean Dip 53
Crispy Candied Noodles 47
Cucumber Relish 37
Egg Rolls 29
Fish Cakes 31
Fried Canapés with Pork Spread 45
Fried Canapés with Prawn Spread 43
Fried Pork Meatballs 39
Fried Stuffed Chicken Wings 33
Fried Sweet Corn Patties 41
Fried Potcrust and Dip 49
Pork and Tomatoe Chilli Dip 51
Pork or Beef Sateh 36
Stuffed Cabbage 56

B

BEEF

Beef Curried in Sweet Peanut Sauce 111
Fried Sun Dried Beef 181
Massaman Curry 99
Savory Beef Salad 71
Stewed Beef 197
Stir-Fried Beef in Oyster Sauce 161
Thai Beef Curry 107

C

CHICKEN

Chicken and Wax Gourd Curry   119
Chicken in Red Curry with Bamboo Shoots   101
Chicken in Sauce on Rice   189
Chicken with Rice Cooked in Chicken Broth   191
Coconut Milk Chicken Soup   61
Fried Stuffed Chicken Wings   33
Massaman Curry   99
Savory Chopped Chicken Salad   69
Savory Stir-Fried Chicken   155
Sour and Spicy Chicken Soup   59
Southern Style Braised Chicken   109
Spicy Barbecued Chicken Salad   73
Spicy Pork, Prawn and Chicken Salad   77
Spicy Stir-Fried Chicken or Pork   149
Steamed Curried Pork, Chicken or Fish   103
Stir Fried Chicken with Cashew Nuts   169
Stir-Fried Chicken with Long Eggplant   165
Stir-Fried Chicken with Water Chestnuts   147
Stuffed Chicken Wings in Pha-naeng Sauce   113
Thai Style Barbecued Chicken   179

CRAB

Stuffed Crab   129

CURRY

Beef Curried in Sweet Peanut Sauce   111
Chicken and Wax Gourd Curry   119
Chicken in Red Curry with Bamboo Shoots   101
Curried Prawns   97
Fish Curry   115
Massaman Curry   99
Red Curry of Duck   117
Red Curry of Mushroom   105
Thai Beef Curry   107

CURRY PASTE

Green Curry Paste   25
Kaeng Khua Curry Paste   24
Massaman Curry Paste   23
Red Curry Paste   26
Phrik Khing Curry Paste   154
Sour Soup Curry Paste   25
Roasted Chilli Sauce (paste) 23
Yellow Curry Paste   24

D

DRINKS

Thai Style Coffee or Tea   217

DUCK

Baked Stuffed Duck   173
Crispy Duck   175
Red Curry of Duck   117

F

FISH

Fish Cakes   31
Fish Curry   115
Fish Flavored Vegetable Soup   77
Fried Sun-Dried Kingfish   145
Fried White Pompano   134
Rock Cod Baked in Banana Leaf   121
Sea Perch Steamed with Chilli in Lime Sauce   123
Steamed Curried Pork, Chicken or Fish   103
Steamed Fish   146
Steamed Pompano with Pickled Plum   135

L

LOBSTER

Charcoal Broiled Lobster with Savory Sauce   125
Broiled Lobster in Tamarind Sauce   95

N

NOODLES

Baked Prawns and Mungbean Noodles   141
Crispy Candied Noodles   47
Mungbean Noodle Soup   65
Spicy Mungbean Noodle Salad   81
Stir Fried Rice Noodles and Prawns   185
Thai Fried Noodles   183
Vermicelli and Fish Sauce   200
Vermicelli and Prawn Sauce   201

P

PORK

Barbecued Pork   177
Barbecued Spareribs   181
Beaten Egg Steamed with Pork   127
Boiled Fresh Ham with Five Spices   157
Fried Canapés with Pork Spread   45
Fried Pork Meatballs   39
Fried Rice With Pork, Shrimp and Egg   187
Massaman Curry   99
Piquant Chopped Pork Salad   85
Pork and Tomatoe Chilli Dip   51
Pork or Beef Sateh   36
Savory Baked Pork Salad   79
Savory Chopped Pork Salad   68
Savory Stir-Fried Pork with Yard-long Beans   154
Spicy Pork, Prawn and Chicken Salad   77
Spicy Stir-Fried Chicken or Pork   149
Steamed Curried Pork, Chicken or Fish   103
Stewed Pork   159
Stir-Fried Bean Sprouts and Crisp-Fried Roasted Pork Belly   171
Stir-Fried Pork with Red Curry Paste   151
Stuffed Cabbage   56
Sweet and Sour Pork   139
Sweet and Sour Spareribs   137

PRAWNS

Baked Prawns and Mungbean Noodles   141
Beaten Egg Steamed with Pork (and Prawns)   127
Curried Prawns   97
Fried Canapés with Prawn Spread   43
Fried Rice with Pork, Shrimp and Egg   187
Garlic Prawns   93
Prawns Steamed with Soy Sauce   143
Savory Prawn Salad   84
Sour and Spicy Prawn Soup   59
Spicy Pork, Prawn and Chicken Salad   77
Stir-Fired Prawns in Tamarind Sauce   92
Stir-Fried Prawns with Vegetables   167
Stir-Fried Rice Noodles and Prawns   185

R

RICE

Chicken in Sauce on Rice   189
Chicken with Rice Cooked in Chicken Broth   191
Chinese Sausage Steamed in Rice   195
Fried Rice with Pork, Shrimp and Eggs   187
Fried Potcrust (rice) and Dip   49
Stir Fried Rice and Shrimp Paste   193

S

SALAD

Papaya Salad   91
Piquant Chopped Pork Salad   85
Savory Baked Pork Salad   79
Savory Beef Salad   71
Savory Chopped Chicken Salad   69
Savory Chopped Pork Salad   68
Savory Prawn Salad   84
Southern Thai Salad   89
Spicy Barbecued Chicken Salad   73
Spicy Mungbean Noodle Salad   81
Spicy Pork, Prawn and Chicken Salad   77
Spicy Squid Salad   75
Spicy Winged Bean Salad   87

SAUCE

Cucumber Relish   37
Egg Roll Sauce   29
Fermented Soybean Sauce   191
Marmalade Sauce   43
Peanut Sweet Chilli Sauce   31
Roasted Chilli Sauce   23
Sateh Sauce (peanut sauce)   36
Sweet Chilli Sauce   179
Sweet and Sour Sauce   137

SHRIMP (see Prawns)

SOUP

Cha Am Sour Tamarind Soup   57
Coconut Milk Chicken Soup   61
Fish Flavored Vegetable Soup   63
Mungbean Noodle Soup   65
Sour and Spicy Chicken Soup   59
Sour and Spicy Prawn Soup   59

SQUID

Sauteed Stuffed Squid   131
Spicy Squid Salad   75

STEAMED:

Beaten Egg Steamed with Pork   127
Chinese Sausage Steamed in Rice   195
Prawns Steamed with Soy Sauce   143
Sea Perch Steamed with Chilli in Lime Sauce   123
Steamed Curried Pork, Chicken or Fish   103
Steamed Fish   146
Steamed White Pompano with Pickled Plum   135

STIR FRIED

Savory Stir-Fried Chicken   155
Spicy Stir-Fried Chicken or Pork   149
Stir-Fried Bean Sprouts and Crisp-Fried Roasted Pork Belly   171
Stir-Fried Beef in Oyster Sauce   161
Stir-Fried Chicken with Cashew Nuts   169
Stir-Fried Chicken with Long Eggplant   165
Stir-Fried Chicken with Water Chestnuts   147
Stir-Fried Kai Lan in Oyster Sauce   163
Stir-Fried Pork with Red Curry Paste   151
Savory Stir-Fried Pork with Yard-long Beans   154
Stir-Fried Prawns in Tamarind Sauce   92
Stir-Fried Prawns with Vegetables   167
Stir-Fried Rice Noodles and Prawns   185

SUN DRIED

Fried Sun Dried Beef   181
Fried Sun Dried King Fish   145

SWEETS

Banana and Glutinous Rice Steamed in Banana Leaf   213
Bananas in Coconut Cream   209
Candied Sweet Potatoe   211
Coconut Milk Ice Cream   215
Corn Pudding in Coconut Cream   209
Fried Bananas   213
Mungbeans in Syrup   208
Sweet Potatoes in Syrup   211
Taro Coconut Custard   205
Thai Style Tapioca   203

T

TAMARIND

Broiled Lobster in Tamarind Sauce   95
Cha Am Sour Tamarind Soup 57
Stir-Fried Prawns in Tamarind Sauce   92

V

VEGETABLE

Fried Sweet Corn Patties   41
Red Curry of Mushrooms   105
Spicy Winged Bean Salad   87
Stir-Fried Kai Lan in Oyster Sauce   163

ASIAN MARKETS LISTING

ARIZONA

Kimbong Market
502 D. Dobson Rd.
Meza, AZ 85202

Siam Import Market
5008 W. Northern Ave. No. 3
Glendale, AZ 85301

CALIFORNIA

American-Chinese Market
1609 W. 7th St.
Los Angeles, CA 90017

Asia Market
9509 Van Nuys Ave.
Panorama, CA 91402

Asian Super Market
739 E. Anaheim St.
Long Beach, CA 90813

Bangkok Market
4757 Melrose Ave.
Los Angeles, CA 90029

Bangkok Grocery
3838 Geary Blvd.
San Francisco, CA 94118

Bangluck Market
5170 Hollywood Blvd
Hollywood, CA 90027

Boonreang Market
473 S. Brookhurst
Anaheim, CA 92804

Canton Food Inc.
1100 E. 5th St.
Los Angeles, CA 90013

Cathay Supermarket
3969 Beverly Blvd.
Los Angeles, CA 90004

Hoa Binh Market
437 E. Holt Ave.
Pomona, CA 91767

Intra Market
1361 E. Colorado St.
Glendale, CA 91205

Kim Hoa Oriental Market
7227 De Soto Ave.
Canoga Park, CA 91306

Man Wah Supermarket
758-762 New High St.
Los Angeles, CA 90012

Oriental Grocery
5527 Del Amo Blvd.
Lakewood, CA 90713

Oriental Mart
11827 Del Amo Blvd.
Cerritos, CA 90701

Siam West Oriental Grocery
9234 Pertaluma Hill Road
Santa Rosa, CA 95404

Sunshine Market
3345 E Artesia Blvd
Long Beach, CA 90805

Thai Market
3826 West Lane
Stockton, CA 95204

Thai Cottage Market
11268 Ventura Blvd.
Studio City, CA 91604

Thai Laos Store
3710-B Westminster
Santa Ana, CA 92703

Vientiane Market
233 Jones St.
San Francisco, CA 94102

COLORADO

K. Grocery
4966 Leetsdale
Denver, CO 80222

Krung Thai Grovery
10146 Montview Blvd.
Aurona, CO 80010

Oriental Food Market
2707 Arapahae Ave.
Boulder, CO 80302

FLORIDA

Asian Market
3214 9th St. N.
St. Petersburg, FL 33704

Far East Grocery
14616 66th St. N.
Clearwater, FL 33546

International Market
1033 9th St. N.
St. Petersburg, FL 33701

Tampa Oriental Super Market
6002 S. Dale Mabry Hwy
Tampa, Fl 33611

Thai Market
916 Harrelson St.
Ft. Walton Beach, FL 32548

Thai market
3323-25 S. Dal Malry Hwy
Tampa, Fl 33609

GEORGIA

Lim's Oriental Food
4887 Memorial Dr. Stone Min
Atlanta, GA 30319

Thai Oriental Market
6767 Highway 85
Riverdale, GA 30274

HAWAII

Asian Grocery
1362 S. Beretania St.
Honolulu, HI 96814

Siam Panich Grocery
171 N. Beretania St.
Honolulu, HI 96813

ILLINOIS

Bangkok Grocery
1003-5 W. Leland Ave.
Chicago, Il 60640

Thai Grocery
5014 N. broadway Ave.
Chicago, IL 60640

Thai Market
4654 N. Western Ave.
Chicago, IL 60625

INDIANA

N. P. Asia Food
3737 N. Shadeland Ave.
Indianapolis, IN 46226

MARYLAND

Asian Foods Inc.
2301 University Blvd. West
Wheaton, MD 20902

Asian American Grovery
8236 Georgia Ave.
Silver Spring, MD 20910

Bangkok Grocery
412 A. Hunderford Dr.
Rockville, MD 20850

Bangkok Oriental
4917 Suitland Rd.
Suitlan, MD 20746

MINNESOTA

Thai Store
1304 Eastlake St.
Minneapolis, MN 55407

MISSISSIPPI

Oriental Mart
2856-D Pass Rd.
Biloxi, MS 39531

MISSOURI

Jay Asia Food
3232 S. Grand St.
St. Louise, MO 63118

NEBRASKA

Asian Market
2413 Lincoln Rd
Bellevue, NE 68005

Bangkok Oriental
645 S. Loewt
Grand Island, NE 68801

NEVADA

Asia Market
1101 E. Charleston Blvd.
Las Vegas, NV 89104

Chinese Oriental
1801 E. Charleston Blvd.
Las Vegas, NV 89104

International Market
900 E Karen Ave.
Las Vegas, NV 89104

NEW YORK

Bangkok Market
106 Park St.
New York, NY 10013

Siam Market
2754 Broadway
New York, NY 10025

NORTH CAROLINA

Thai Market
122-124 S. Main St.
Spring Lake, NC 28390

OHIO

Bangkok Grocery
3277 Refugee Rd.
Columbus, OH 43227

Thai Grocery
108 E. Main St.
Columbus, OH 43215

OKLAHOMA

Su's Oriental Market
3313 E. 32 Pl.
Tulsa, OK 74135

PENNSYLVANIA

P & P Grocery
4307 Locus St.
Philadelphia, PA 19104

SOUTH CAROLINA

Port of Siam
5400 Hwy. AS.
Myrtle Beach, SC 29577

TEXAS

A. P. Oriental Market
3835 Chesser Boyer Rd.
Ft Worth, TX 76103

American-Asian Foods
6866 Shad Brook Lane
Dallas, TX 75231

Asian Grocery
9191 Forest Lane 3
Dallas, TX 75243

Bangkok Market
3404 Navigation
Houston, TX 77003

Dragon Gate Market
3524 E. Lancaster
Ft. Worth, TX 76103

Laos Grocery
5813 Amarillo Blvd E.
Amarillo, TX 97107

Suvanee's Oriental
7403 Highway 80
W. San Antonio, TX 78227

T. R. Food Market
104 Northwood Shopping
Center
Dallas, TX 75225

Thai Shop
403 E. Commerce
"River Square"
San Antonio, TX 78205

Thailand Market
2216 W. Granwyler
Irving, TX 75061

UTAH

Royal Thai Market
860 W. Riverdale Rd.
Riverdale, UT 84403

K & K International Market
7046 S. State Street
Midvale, UT 84047

VIRGINIA

Backlick Oriental
6681-28 Backlick Rd.
Springfield, VA 22150

Bangkok '54 Oriental
3832 MT. Vernon Ave.
Alexandria, VA 32305

Thai Oriental Market
4807-9 Columbia Pike
Arlington, VA 22204

WASHINGTON

Anger Wat Market
5912-196th S.W. No. K
Lynwood, WA 98036

Asian market
10855 N.E. 85th St.
Bellevue, WA 98004

WISCONSIN

Oriental Grovery
322 E. Main St.
Wakesha, WI 53186

Vientiance Market
12205 16th St.
Milwaukee, WI 53204

ALSO AVAILABLE FROM
SNOW LION GRAPHICS / SLG BOOKS

PRICE

MIPAM by Lama Yongden
     paperback,   ISBN 0-9617066-0-0 $12.95

THE UNVEILING OF LHASA, by Edmund Chandler
     paperback,   ISBN 0-9617066-1-9 $12.95
     hardback,   ISBN 0-9617066-2-7 $14.95

WIND BETWEEN THE WORLDS, by Robert Ford
     paperback,   ISBN 0-9617066-8-6 $12.95
     hardback   ISBN 0-9617066-9-4 $19.95

LANDS OF THE THUNDERBOLT, by Lord Ronaldshay
     paperback,   ISBN 0-0617066-6-X $12.95
     hardback,   ISBN 0-9617066-7-8 $19.95

A TIBETAN ON TIBET, by G. A. Combe
     paperback,   ISBN 0-943389-02-X $12.95

HEALING IMAGE: THE GREAT BLACK ONE, by William Stablein, Ph.D.
     paperback,   ISBN 0-943389-06-2 $14.95

DON'T YOU WANT SOMEBODY TO LOVE?, by Darby Slick
     paperback,   ISBN 0-943389-08-9 $15.95

To order: Add US$1.75 postage for the first volume; 75 cents for each additional volume. California residents add 7%. Postal rates may change. Foreign postal rates are higher. All prices in US dollars. Makes cheque payable to SLG BOOKS.

SLG BOOKS
P.O. BOX 9465
BERKELEY, CA 94709
USA

Tel: 510-841-5525
Fax: 510-841-5537